Volume 2 Returning

Decisions Decisions: Getting Answers to Life's Challenges   Large Print

Haneefa Mateen

Copyright © 2023 by Haneefa Mateen

All rights reserved.

ISBN 978-1-73772-19-5-6

No portion of this book may be reproduced in any form without written permission from the publisher or author, except as permitted by U.S. copyright law.

Disclaimer: The author of this book, Decisions, Decisions' stories, experiences and opinions are from author's perspective and are not intended as medical advice or the use of any techniques as a form of treatment for physical, medical, psychiatric, mental health problems either directly or indirectly. The intent of the author is only to share experiences in a general nature in her quest for emotional and spiritual wellbeing. In the event that you use any of the information in this book for yourself, which is your constitutional right, the author and publisher assumes no responsibility or liability whatsoever for readers or purchasers of this book.

Decisions, Decisions is a non-fiction story, however some names, locations, and other identifying information were changed to protect privacy of individuals.

Book Cover art: Haneefa Mateen

Contents

Introduction	1
PART ONE: Adjusting to the United States	9
Chapter 1: Graduation	10
Chapter 2: Reversed Cultural Shock	19
Chapter 3: Homeless	28
Chapter 4: In the Shelters	38
Chapter 5: Sent Here and There	48
Chapter 6: Men	55
Chapter 7: Gratitude	65
Chapter 8: Healing Emotionally	70

Chapter 9: Spiritual Practices	82
PART TWO: Is There a Home for Me?	95
Chapter 10: A Push Out the Door	96
Chapter 11: Family	103
Chapter 12: Not Again!	121
Chapter 13: Sacred Contracts Archetypes Cards	126
Chapter 14: More Guidance with Sacred Contracts Cards	179
Chapter 15: Where Else to Go?	205
Chapter 16: Home?	216
Books and Articles Mentioned in This Book	228
Author's Bio	232

Introduction

People ask me, "How did you, and still do, go through tough life challenges and can smile?" They want to know what I did to survive. Divination is one of the tools I use.

No need to suffer depression and anxiety worrying what decisions to make, or did you make the right decision. Is it even your decision to make or someone else's? No need to worry what is going to happen in the future, because your guides give you insight into the situation that you are concerned about, and will show you what you have control over and what you don't. Depression and fears often comes from feeling trapped or stuck. Asking for higher guidance for what you can do to improve your situation, through the use of divination gives you solutions and putting that guidance into action, gets you unstuck. It does take faith and courage because what you will be shown is new and different. Or often what you've known all along you need to do.

"Insanity is doing the same thing over and over again and expecting different results." Albert Einstein

Fear of change or what others will think, may have stopped you. Divination gives you encouragement by showing you options. The results often better than you could have ever imagined. Miracles, lots of miracles and abundance happen.

Well, when you start to see less crises in your life, as you understand how the universe functions around you, and make better choices in your thoughts and behaviors, then it is not hard, even for us who are hardheaded, to believe. Especially when your life begins to flow smoothly synchronically, and what you need simply shows up abundantly. Divination provides roadmaps or a GPS that lets you know where the traffic congestion is and guides you through the detours. Sometimes we get stuck in traffic anyway. GPS gives alerts and warnings ahead of time. Divination also gives you alerts and can help you get back on the main road of your life.

It decreases conflicts in relationships by allowing the oracle to show us what's best. From your heart with sincerity, you can ask the following questions: How do I improve myself to have better friendships? Should I share or not? Am I enabling? Or do I tend to be selfish and not know how to share and love? Show me how to feel love and receive love. How do I get along with his or her family? Should we buy this car at this time and from what dealer? Or change employment? Or relocate? Where do I go for guidance when I'm feeling sad or frustrated? If we disagree on what to do, what is best for the whole situation? What prayers do we need for healing? And then follow the guidance, each step of the way. Relationships help us learn, grow and change.

This is not a religious book. I use some foreign language terms because that is the way I learned them and is my way of continuing to honor these indigenous cultures and beliefs. With deep respect for indigenous cultures and the people who truly have the knowledge, I thank them and yield to them.

Religions and holy scriptures threaten human beings with damnation and going to hell for our transgressions, yet doesn't tell or show us <u>how</u> to stay out of hell. Just, "don't this or don't do that," with contradictory messages of "we were born in sin," "confess and you'll be forgiven," and don't let the devil tempt you." To be honest, I've tried and tried to understand the Bible and Quran translated into old English, with stories I can't relate to our current days and times. Religious leaders argue over the meanings. The use of oracles and other forms of divination can show each of us, as well as our communities how to stay out of unnecessary hell in both this life (and the next).

Hopefully this book introduces you to different perspectives as my personal stories bring understanding of how ancient and now popularized practices for making decisions — when used properly — brings improved quality of life, inner peace, satisfaction, and sense of purpose. And is inspirational to you on your own life's journey.

In the first book, <u>Mother's Love from Beyond: A Healing Journey of Grief and Loss</u>, readers learned about my childhood and early adult years, as I was prepared through life experiences to accept that there are many different ways of healing and knowing. Readers gained faith and courage along with me as I learned to trust intuitive higher guidance.

In this book, I offer more tools for you gaining access to your own guidance for your own life, while continuing with my stories from Volume 1, of Decisions Decisions of how I was introduced to these divination tools and how my lifestyle changed along the way. This book is mostly written in the order I learned these techniques however, the stories are updated with my current thoughts, events, and style of writing.

Previous readers asked me to go into more details about my middle years, my thirties, forties, and early fifties to explain how I got from, and transformed through multiple crises and the obstacles I endured described here in Volume 2, from then to now.

My goal with this book, Decisions Decisions, as with my other books in the "Spirituality Made Simple series" is to make spirituality and healing simple. Simple to understand, and simple to apply to daily life.

I use several approaches to meet different readers' needs, interests, and learning styles. Some people learn best from information and research. Other people enjoy and learn from life stories as examples. Here, both approaches are combined. Take what you need and leave the rest. At different times later in your life you may want to come back to this series for more understanding.

PART ONE: Adjusting to the United States

Chapter 1: Graduation

I returned to the School for International Training's (SIT), after a year away in Zimbabwe. The college campus provided me with healing because it was nestled in the tree covered hills of Vermont with the soothing sounds of waterfalls and streams all along the roads. It was a nurturing small community too, but because most of the students and teachers were white, it felt shocking to be surrounded by them, although I knew most of them previously, after me living in African villages.

We had the traditional graduation ceremony with caps and gowns, however, we chose our gowns from a of variety of colors and designs from four different countries. Mine was from Kenya. The faculty giving us our diplomas wore their alumni university gowns and sashes. In the afternoon, our undergraduate World Issues Program had its own separate ceremony where we wore long white Tibetan scarves. My cousin came up from Philadelphia. I was glad to have her there with me. We have a photo of her trying to wrap her Tibetan scarf. She received her doctorate degree a few weeks later. Laughing, she accurately described the SIT campus as the, "hippie college on the hill."

I had to decide where I would live after graduation. Having brought most of my belongings with me and put them in campus storage, I would have to ship them to wherever city my new home would be. My grandmother was begging me to come live with her in Philadelphia. Stay in Vermont? Should I go back to the Midwest city where I grew up, where my closest siblings live? Continuing my education at the master's level or working in other cities was tempting but I missed my family and friends after being away from them for two years. Return to Chicago which was only a couple of train or greyhound bus's hours away from them? I did I Ching readings on all of these relocation possibilities:

***

From SIT to Philadelphia?

Hexagram 28 (line 5) into hexagram 32.

Hexagram 28 is an unbalanced situation or attitude. Line 5: Have to be able to adapt and be flexible with the current realities of the situation.

Hexagram 32 Duration indicates making a commitment to continuous striving towards goals throughout adversity and challenges. This is easier when you are able to adapt to changing situations and your upmost goal is spiritual growth of improving your own character and harmony in all relationships with others, both family and career.

∗∗∗

From SIT to the Midwest city where I grew up and worked? Hexagram 50 The Caldron Transformation (lines 2 and 6) into hexagram 62 Deficiency.

Hexagram 50 represents spiritual power with the emotional and mental development of spiritual transformation of self and society. This begins with letting go of old obsolete, no longer useful beliefs, behaviors, and goals. Focus is on learning alternative spiritual perspectives and approaches to solving societal concerns. Allowing the oracles and divination to guide you. Line 2: Others may disapprove of your personal transformative changes. Line 6: After doing personal inner development, you can be of service to the community. A hexagram 62 situation is not the time to push forward or be ambitious. Will have limited resources and energy.

From SIT to Chicago?

Hexagram 8 Unity (line 4) into hexagram 45 Gathering Together.

Hexagram 8 is about finding and joining with others in a small group. This requires commitment and perseverance and a proper leader who can balance the needs of the individual with the needs of the group. It is important to not hesitate too long in joining because you will miss out on bonding, as well as growth, while the group develops. Hexagram 45 is a large community gathering together that is influenced by the divine and our unseen ancestors for us to come together. Oracles and divination are used to guide and govern the community.

Chicago seemed the best destination of all my choices. This was based on my limited understanding of the spiritual readings and about life at that time.

Back in Chicago, again surrounded by the tall apartment buildings and concrete, I did not feel so desperately constrained and separated from nature. It was as if my soul was satisfied after having found my people and my culture. Determined to keep that sense of wholeness I gained in Zimbabwe and maintain it, I vowed to bring this culture back with me to the United States and share this from inside me with others no matter what, not to be stolen from me again.

Remember, the I Ching Hexagram 55 Abundance was my initial reading inquiring about my purpose and role while I was in Zimbabwe back in 1996?

While in Zimbabwe and at SIT, I did experience true abundance. But I guess I forgot about the other part of the hexagram 55 advice and forewarning of decline. What goes up so high must come down. Similar to what happens after profound creative, healing, and spiritual experiences, after feeling so blissfully wonderful we must then bring the lessons we learned back into everyday life. To do this we must face the realities of our lives internally, as well as in our surrounding environments and communities.

In contrast to feeling bliss, Earthly life can feel harsh and painful. I had made an inner vow of bringing back with me to the United States, the true love and community life given to me in Zimbabwe. How was I to hold onto that love and peace and share it? Life was about to test me to the umpteenth degree more than I could have ever imagined!

Chapter 2: Reversed Cultural Shock

I was happy to be back in the United States. Readjusting, however was rough. Although the SIT counselor talked to our classes about culture shock before we went abroad and reverse culture shock when we returned to campus, I was still not prepared for the intensity of reversed culture shock. Perhaps because the Zimbabweans were true to their word that they would not let me get homesick, and while I did have to adjust to a new language and culture, it didn't shock me as much. My only clue for missing the United States was when, in the last two months I started wanting junk food like pizza and potato chips. I didn't even usually eat pizza, because of my gluten and dairy intolerance, I couldn't eat the crust nor the cheese. I did miss the crunch of plain potato chips, since the potato chips sold in snack bags in Zimbabwe had vinegar and were soft. A friend shipped a box to me with the ingredients for my favorite comfort food, homemade rice flour pancakes, the month before I returned to the United States. And yes, yes I was missing and looking forward to seeing my family and friends that I hadn't seen for almost three years.

In Chicago, my friend, Sandra invited me to live with her temporarily at her two-bedroom apartment. Everyone was glad to see me initially. However, they didn't understand or recognize how much I had grown and changed. Their lives had changed too, but I was expecting that we could still do the same activities we did before I left. They got tired of me excitedly talking about Zimbabwe. A friend who went to West Africa, and I were able to share stories, but she was only away for a month. I talked about Zimbabwe so much that people asked me, "Why didn't you stay in Africa?" For some reason, that possibility never crossed my mind. In my naïvety, I only automatically thought to finish my classes and assignments on campus, then go home to my family.

I was hoping my village experiences with being authentic and loving would help us be even closer, but instead I lost friends. Some told me that I didn't have common sense. Of course, I no longer had common sense because I was readjusting to the American society, it's routines, materialism, wastefulness and faster pace with no time to do much together with anyone. When walking down the street greeting people, people would look at me crazy for saying hello to them and asking them how they were doing. People seemed cold, self-absorbed and fake.

"She talks too slow and moves too slow." That is what a job interviewer for a nursing position at a hospital kidney dialysis unit told my nurse friend, who suggested I try there. Another interviewer said, "I see you've had 12 sick days in a year."

She judged me not knowing that I had heard a recommendation that it is the best for everyone to take "mental health days" instead of needing to take sick days off." I purposely started taking the day off before my period when I was quietly crabby and achy. Previously I rarely took vacation days, nor sick days, nor holidays. Raised a Muslim I didn't celebrate Christmas or Easter, so I volunteered to allow coworkers time off with their families. Plus, we got time and a half pay for holidays. Other people regularly bragged about calling in sick for sports games, or just because it was a beautiful sunny day, or because they partied too much the night before and had difficulty getting up the next morning. I didn't take sick days, instead accruing a nice bonus check at the end of each year, until I heard about self-care.

But the interviewers didn't know how dedicated a worker I am. All they saw in front of them was a tall, too skinny, African American woman who they probably thought was on drugs. Who had been on a strict vegan, gluten-free diet too long. That walked for miles and miles, two hours up and down the rocky terrain of Zimbabwe hills, only having had a single plate of mealie meal with a large spoonful of collard greens. Maybe if she had eaten the moponi worms and the smelly dried fish she would've had more protein, more muscle, more energy and thought clearer. Depressed with homesickness and daydreaming for the land and loving villagers she left behind. Who didn't know yet, that she had done possible irreversible damage to her body.

Unaware of how I appeared to others, I of course took this rejection personally, sinking me into depression as my friends pressured me to keep seeking employment. In some ways, I actually felt better physically than than I felt before I went to Zimbabwe and while I was in Zimbabwe. Perhaps because other than walking, I didn't do heavy labor. I did quietly get chest pain when I tried hoeing in the garden with the women or helping with digging wells with a shovel. But somehow the villagers knew and didn't ask me to participate more than a couple of times.

Back in the United States, difficulty climbing stairs was my first warning sign that something was wrong with my health. The closer I got to the top of the stairs, the more my legs felt heavy as if I could barely pick them up, and I was short of breath with mild chest pains. Because I had a history of a diagnosis of asthma that's what I thought the problem was. And so did doctors when I finally went to Cook County hospital emergency room, feeling like someone stuck an ice pick in my chest sharp pains when I tried to inhale deeply, along with the constant aching pressure in my heart. I was weak, dizzy when standing up and walking. Breathing in cold air or drinking cold liquids also intensified my heart area pain. Yet I didn't think about how irrational it was at the time, to get on buses and then two subway trains from the Southside, and through the snow to get to Cook County hospital. How I did it, was probably from sheer will, same as how I've made it through all the other crises in my life.

Without employment, I spent many days alone at home. Deeper depression was sure to follow, and it did, giving people even more reasons to be concerned, yet stay away. Only years later did I learn that these are normal symptoms of reverse culture shock, especially for people like me who were immersed in village culture and lived far away longer.

Chapter 3: Homeless

Unable to achieve employment, my stay with Sandra lasted beyond the six months allowed on her lease. Plus like me, she was more of a loner, and she desperately wanted her privacy back. A mutual friend Paula, put my belongings in storage and helped me search the newspaper advertising for an apartment of my own. She found a room up north, then she paid my rent and drove me there. The rooming house was close to a few major streets with plenty of stores and restaurants. Paula also gave me money for food and to call her from time to time on outside pay phones. It was winter, and I trudged through Chicago's usual first week of January blizzard leftover snow.

My friend Paula had only paid for two month's rent. So in February 1999, I went to the Department of Human Services to ask if they would give me a month's rent so that I would not be evicted. The older woman behind the desk asked me some questions and had me fill out some forms. And then she talked on and on and on about everything else. She didn't think that my heart symptoms would qualify me for a medical card. She knew because her daughter also had a heart problem. At the end, the most I understood is that I did not qualify for the program because I didn't have a regular monthly income.

Next, I went across the street to an unemployment program inside a church. I had called earlier. It was located in the basement. They were just closing and gave me a business card to call for an appointment. I thought, how can I call for an appointment without money? I had walked a long way to get there.

An old man came up to me and asked me if I would like to join him for lunch. I followed him to one of the circular tables and sat down. There was a younger man and two other women at the table. They asked me why I was there. I expressed my frustration and fear of not knowing where I was going to live next month. The young man started telling me about the different social services in the area and offered to show me some of them.

After lunch, I followed him around for the remainder of the afternoon. He led me a few blocks away to the Salvation Army building. The offices didn't open until 1:00 PM. Around the back of the building, lunches were also served at the Salvation Army, so we ate a second lunch there. We stood in a long line that wound around the building and up a tall steep flight of stairs. There were more stairs inside. The portions on our plates were small. With my limited wheat-free and mostly vegetarian diet, I had even less to choose from. I ate the canned fruits and vegetables. After eating, we went inside a side door, where again I waited a long time sitting on a hard plastic chair in the waiting area to see a case manager, only to be told that I needed to go to the Salvation Army on Belmont Avenue that was closer to where I was rooming.

Back out on the street, we talked as we walked. He showed me the overnight shelters in the area. There were two shelters for women. One was in the church basement that was affiliated with R.E.S.T., an acronym for Residence for Effective Shelter Transitions, and required a ticket to get in. The other shelter located a few blocks away, was open on a first come, first serve basis. He and I ate a delicious free dinner that night. It was getting dark, I needed to walk home. He told me to return early in the morning to speak with someone at R.E.S.T., which is an acronym for residence for affective shelter transition. It was located on the fourth floor of the building that I went to for employment services and ate lunch and met the young man who was kind enough to show me around the area. I had to be there the next morning before 9:00, since I did not have an appointment.

I signed in with the receptionist but did not have to wait long before my name was called. A counselor, who introduced herself as Jennifer, led me towards the back to a room full of cubicles. After asking me questions while she filled out a stack of forms, she told me I could get a room soon. As long as I stayed in either of the two women shelters, all I had to do is go to scheduled meetings there at REST and in the community. She handed me a sheet of paper to sign my name, where she had circled the meetings that I was interested in, such as the women's group on Monday and a women's art group on Wednesday mornings. There were also meetings that were required for everyone to attend. She also gave me a list of alcoholic and narcotics anonymous meetings in the neighborhood. She told me that the more meetings I attended, the sooner I will be placed in housing. So although I never had a substance-abuse addiction, I could go to those meetings too. Years ago, I went to Adult Children of Alcoholics' meetings, therefore I was familiar with the twelve step anonymous programs.

Jennifer called and made appointments for me while I was there. She had asked me about any history of domestic violence, so she set me up with a domestic violence support group, and for a mental health assessment later that week. She also told me where the local public aid office was.

The next day I went to the Salvation Army on Belmont Avenue, and to my surprise they agreed to arrange for one month's rent, and also gave me a $25 voucher for the Salvation Army thrift store. My friend Paula had only given me money for January and February's rent, this would pay rent for March. After that, she informed me that she could no longer help.
I went "home" and packed my large denim backpack. My plan was to spend nights in a shelter and walk the twenty blocks "home" after scheduled daytime

meetings to nap or shower, then walk back to the shelters. This proved to be quite an undertaking because I had to walk to get to everywhere. It was very cold outside. Other homeless people taught me that there were free meals served at different places at different times, on different days of the week. I could count on breakfasts and lunches at the Salvation Army. There was an additional lunch on Tuesdays and Thursdays in the basement where REST was. Other days I could get lunch at the community center. Big bowls of soup and bread were served for dinner at the large Saint James Church's basement located a few blocks west of REST. Besides mealtimes, I had to keep track of the new appointments Jennifer made for me and find out where they were located, since I was unfamiliar with the north side of Chicago.

Chapter 4: In the Shelters

My biggest challenge was actually getting into and surviving being in the shelter. The REST women's shelter did not open until 9:00 PM, and card holders were allowed in first. Rarely were there any beds left. I am glad that someone told me about the community center women's shelter, which opened earlier in the evening, so I did not have to stand outside in the cold too long. Being chilled has always made me feel sick and miserable. The first night I arrived at the community center, when I signed in I had to answer the same emotionally painful personal questions again. Then I was sent upstairs. The upstairs was dimly lit, but I saw rows and rows of bunkbeds with women and children. I was told to go back downstairs. The woman who registered me, thought I was a teenager although I was 42 years old at the time! She directed me to sit at one of the round tables with the rest of the women. I followed them to the kitchen for a late dinner. The food was surprisingly tasty and abundant. Then we were each given a number for one of the fifty, closely spaced, exercise mats on the floor. One of the volunteers brought me a small white sheet and a gray army blanket.

My mat was along the main walkway going to the bathroom. The floor was hard and cold. Women kept getting up during the night to go to the bathroom. Then there were stragglers, most of them were intoxicated but were allowed in late anyway. Since the mats were only a few inches apart, some women who were easily irritated by the slightest bump by the person next to them would start arguments. Others would steal, so I had to sleep with one eye open. My mat was also located near the noisy ice machine, so I got very little sleep at night. Just when I was starting to fall asleep, someone would go to the bathroom or turn a shower on. All too soon, it was 6 o'clock and the staff was waking us up to get ready to leave at 6:30 AM! There were only two sinks in the bathroom for all the women, so I didn't even try to wash up. Breakfast was served. I grabbed a

CHAPTER 4: IN THE SHELTERS

quick bite to eat and back out on the street I went.

Being out on the streets was very frightening to me. Since my parents keep me indoors and as an adult I was usually a homebody, I was not street smart. Most of the other homeless people looked hard and mean to me. There were frequent fights breaking out in front of me on the sidewalks, especially when we were together in waiting rooms and soup kitchens. After prayer service at the Salvation Army, they would serve us breakfast. The Salvation Army had a warming center that opened at 10:00 AM. This meant walking the streets until then. When it opened, we had to go through a metal detector and be searched by a security guard with a handheld metal detector. The security guard stayed at the entrance of a large room filled with chairs around small tables with games to play. There was also a television. Most of the programs on the television were educational. This turned out to be a quiet, safe place.

Quiet and safe but I felt uncomfortable surround by mostly men everywhere I went. I was friendly, polite and courteous, unlike a lot of the other women. My smile also made me attractive, but I got tired of being bombarded with personal questions because I wasn't interested having a boyfriend. I had enough problems of my own! So when I was told about a warming center just for women, I was eager to go there, but I had to wait until it opened at 1:00 PM.

CHAPTER 4: IN THE SHELTERS

The women's warming circle was located on the second floor of a large building on the corner of Lawrence and Sheridan Road. As I waited for the elevator, in the main lobby, I noticed to my left the entrance to the Cultural Center. Ironically, I had traveled there from the Southside of Chicago for a job interview the year before. They told me there were no paying jobs available. Now I rode the elevators up to the second floor with tears in my eyes. Women were already lined up along the white painted hallway. We were buzzed through the security door with the glass window, into a large sunlight room that also had white walls. When I signed in, I noticed there were over 60 signatures from the day before. The staff who greeted me were pleasant, and again I had to answer questions about my personal life. They took me on a tour. There were washers and dryers, a storage room with toiletries, bathroom with showers, kitchen and separate small support group meeting rooms. The main large room had shelves with books, games, puzzles and craft items. It also had a television and was filled with small tables and chairs. Snacks were served that day. Other days, dinner was served in the evening. The warming center closed at 8 PM, from there we would leave back out into the cold night to go to the shelters.

All of these interviews at these different social service agencies were very emotionally difficult I felt ashamed and humiliated having to ask for help. One interview location was very claustrophobic and frightening, sitting face-to-face close enough for our knees to almost touch, being asked questions about past abuse by a tall African American male worker that kept staring at me. Gratefully, a white lady was there too taking notes. There was no introduction as to what the interview was for, and no real explanation of the results at the end. And no place to cry after the intake sessions. Just left open and raw.

That night was horrible as memories flashed before my eyes while I tried to hold back the painful feelings and details of past abuse. On top of the emotional pain, I also couldn't sleep because of the burning pains from my waist to the soles of my feet and now my hands. My lower back, abdomen, neck and head were also aching. Eventually dozing off, I woke up late, not wanting to get up and face the day. Lying there, I realized I had an overwhelming feeling of being trapped. Trapped not only during my teenage years because I didn't know any better, but also now because I didn't know what my options were, and I was again in a very desperate vulnerable position at the mercy of others. Used to my needs verbally rejected over and over again when I did ask for help. How could I have had any energy left to face the rejection of not being hired for jobs again and again?

I felt in a daze, shocked state from all the new information that I had to learn and remember for survival. The sidewalks, waiting rooms and other places I had to go to for

appointments seemed filled with mean looking and hardened street people.
I do not remember ever again seeing that young man who helped me the first day. There were other men who helped me on other days to find where I needed to go. Women were distant, mistrustful and competitive. This made me feel fearful and vulnerable. Some women rudely asked me why I was always smiling. I guess smiling and being courteous was my defense mechanism, and it did help to get me things that I needed.

Chapter 5: Sent Here and There

The following weeks, I had to go to appointments from which other appointments were scheduled, so that I had appointments almost every day. I did not qualify for the mental health services at ACCESS, so I was sent to the community counseling center located about six blocks west of REST. I was assigned a psychiatrist and a social worker. After an assessment there, it was determined that I should also go to the Quetzal Center. The Quetzal Center was for sexual abuse counseling. It was located almost a mile away, to the north. I had to walk there too. Luckily as long as I had the official REST sheet of paper signed, all my appointments counted towards points for housing. In addition, I still had to go to the mandatory meetings at REST.

The mandatory meetings at REST were boring, mostly because the repetitive topics did not apply to me. For example, almost every week at the Tuesday Housing Group, and the Immediate Support Group on Thursday mornings, we were given the same budget forms to fill out. Having worked the most of my life and a bread winner in both of my marriages, I had always been good at budgeting my money. I split my paychecks three ways – a third went to pay bills, another third went to the bank for savings, and the rest I can spend if I chose to. At the meetings there were limited participation by the other clients. There was always at least one person who was loud, negatively aggressive, talkative and tried to take up the whole meeting time. The facilitators seemed like they were afraid of these clients and rarely intervened. Women's Self-Support Group on Monday afternoons was interesting, when we could get discussions going.

The group that I really liked was Women's Art Group on Wednesdays. As a lover of arts and crafts since I was a young child, I probably would have made the best of the time anyway, but there were several reasons that I especially liked the Women's Art Group. One, there were plenty of art supplies and we were asked which other supplies we would like. The cost didn't matter. Two, although the facilitator Brian was a young man, he commanded respect and provided structure and compassion. He was during ministry from Uptown Baptist Church, but he didn't preach to us. He was a walking, living example of Christian teachings. Three, he took us on field trips to art galleries and treated us to lunch afterwards at restaurants. For example, we went to the Norman Rockwell exhibit at the Chicago Historical Society. At $15 a ticket, it would've been difficult for us to afford it. Yet, he paid our way, and still took us to lunch afterwards.

Health Talk group, on Thursday afternoons was interesting mostly because I am a registered nurse, and personally interested in a healthy lifestyle. I actually learned some new information there. Then every weekday afternoon from 2:00 to 3:00 PM REST had Alcohol Anonymous, or Cocaine Anonymous, or Narcotics Anonymous meetings. I went to these meetings there, and at the local hospitals in the evenings and weekends. The readings from the twelve step Big Books, along with personal testimonies were inspirational even though I did not have a substance abuse problem.

My goal was to get as many signatures as possible so that I could get a room or apartment sooner. I still worried and had nightmares about losing my belongings, often crying and lying awake from 1:00 AM. It was very scary and depressing watching homeless women try to carry around their remaining possessions. Many had mentally illness or were on drugs, which I was afraid I would become too if I were totally homeless. I'd lose my mind because I would no longer have a reason for living. Even though previously, after my near death experience and especially after living in rural African villages where there was extreme poverty, I had thought I had not valued possessions and I could do with less. Now, I really did not want to do away with the few belongings I do have left. Probably because what remains of what I have, and if I could have my own apartment would represent my independence, identity, and potential creativity, plus stability and having my life and my belongings organized.

Chapter 6: Men

My other challenge was the men. I've always tried to speak to everyone with respect, having friendly conversations about the weather or homelessness, and recovery in an honest manner. But the men all wanted more, asking me personal questions immediately. They would get offended when they see or hear that I "talk to someone else."
A potential for fights between other men and girlfriends, which of course I would know nothing about. Even with me being upfront and honest. They had only one thing on their minds – sex. They tell me, "You're beautiful and

fresh." They would say they want to marry me or shack up with me. All of which kept my abuse issues on the surface, and me struggling to stay on top of depression and my sanity.

Now I really tried to be open to, or perhaps deluding myself into believing that all men are not "bad" and that sex is not what they want from me, hoping they just wanted conversation and companionship. But then some would cling, following me everywhere I went, having me change my plans or theirs. No, I couldn't just leave them at the dinner table! And they just didn't get it, when I tried to explain.

I was too through when an older man asked me while we were walking down the sidewalk, "Is the hair on the rest of your body as pretty and thick as the hair on your head? And is it long enough to braid!"

I gave him a mean look, but he went on talking about trying to figure out how he could get a place where I could move in with him. It didn't matter how many times I had told him I was not interested in a relationship with any man, and talking to someone for two days was not enough time to get to know someone enough to invite them in. His feelings were hurt when I went on and went to the library, after telling him that I planned to spend the morning at the library and then had important business to take care of. I was glad that I left him at the other building, although I apologized and stated that it was not my intention to ditch him. But inside myself, I knew I had to find a way to get away from him, after he also complained that, I "left the lunchroom with another man."

There was another young man, I had only met the day before at an Narcotics Anonymous meeting who thought it was perfectly okay to hold my hand and hug me. Well, I will return hugs at a meeting but when he offered to carry my bag and then hugged me in front of all the ladies near the entrance of the drop-in center, it might have gotten me in trouble with them. Previously I'd talked to men for longer times during the day, and none had inappropriately put their hands on me. Other men were also watching probably thinking that I have a different man every day. Jealousy could be dangerous!

Subsequently I stopped going to the lunchroom to eat and to outside AA or NA meetings. I needed the calories and I needed meetings signed on my attendance sheet, but I didn't need the sexual harassment. Yes, I'm recovering from abuse. But no woman should have to put up with harassment even if it is "sincere." The men have no idea what it feels like. They were in recovery hopefully, but the addictive behavior was still there. They were needy and needed their self-esteem boosted, but I wasn't the one! After that whenever men offered to pay my way, house my large backpack or me —I declined.

Not all homeless people or men are that way of course. One man showed me a store that I could go to exchange food stamps for cash. I did it twice.

However, when I saw that it was only a small amount of cash that the store owner gave me, I stopped, especially because this then meant that I couldn't buy groceries either. I needed the cash to pay my credit card off, which I did in a few months. Having always prided myself on paying my bills on time, I felt ashamed. After that I had no cash. No cash for toilet paper nor sanitary napkins. It was humiliating.

Love Me Love Me Not

There are several ways to ask the oracles about getting into relationships with other people. This includes friendships and romantic relationships. From Ausar Auset Society Church classes, I learned how to make healthier choices.

In separate readings, you could use the oracle cards or I Ching coins to ask, "What would my strengths and weaknesses be in a relationship with? "What would the prospective friend's strengths and weaknesses be in a relationship with me?" "How can we help each other grow emotionally and spiritually?"

I asked: Please assist with divine guidance and insight into the relationship between James and I, and the effect on my incarnation objective destiny purpose:

Metu Neter Cards: Heru tem tchaas (-)/ Auset tem tchaas (-). This means there could be a good relationship between husband and wife, except that both these cards are negative. We really didn't know what a healthy was.

It was true that there was conflicts, angry words, instability, my lack of will and commitment. I would've said no to having anything to do with James, or any man, except that the I Ching reading urged me to give him a chance. Plus I needed to have a man by my side for protection from the other men. I switched from a tall 6'2" stocky built macho man Mike to a short, thin, clingy, less threatening James. Both were a few years older than I. Initially, the taller Mike tried to fight and chase away James, but James stood his ground.

The I Ching guidance was similar but more positive. Hexagram 8 Union is a time to come together and hold together. The individual personal needs must not be neglected for benefit of the union. It's best not to hesitate to join, otherwise you will suffer accordingly. Or if you're already in the situation, but don't do what you're supposed to do. Do what needs to be done, to make it work.

So I inquired again of the cards. If James and I are to unite, what energies are needed to improve the relationship:

Metu Neter cards: Het Heru tu maat (+)/ Tehuti tu tchaas (+). Being able to express joy and experience pleasure, along with having faith and optimism, while following wise counsel and regular use of the oracles.

I followed up with doing I Ching readings every two months. Hexagram 53, Gradual Progress (line 1) means I'm new, inexperienced and therefore will make mistakes and get criticism, but this is good as we learn from mistakes. Our relationship changed to being peaceful when we were together, as I gradually learned to listen to James, instead of trying to insert my opinion, or insisting on being right. In return, James was the first man to actually give and not take from me. He considered my needs and brought me useful gifts. It was his unreasonable jealousy that caused arguments. Although it was a platonic, celibate relationship James was afraid that I would cheat the same as his first wife did. We both had to learn to trust each other.

Please Note: The I Ching interpretations and insights came from reading several I Ching books, listed in the back of this book, which I used to summarize the main points here and in later chapters.

Chapter 7: Gratitude

Two months later, through their transitional housing program, REST gave me a room in the Northmere apartment building. It was nicknamed affectionately, "The Nightmare" because at night you could hear people crying, screaming, some tenants knocking on each room's door begging for cigarettes. Although it was only one small room, and I shared an adjoined bathroom with another woman and roaches it was my space, safe and warm. No more having to walk the streets in the cold, waiting for the shelters to open, hoping there was room for one more. Initially, I did have to continue walking to the now further away soup kitchens. However, as staff and new friends saw that my walking was becoming increasingly more difficult, they gave me a little refrigerator and started bringing meals to me.

Jennifer used a REST agency van to go over to the Southside of Chicago and bring me my belongings out of storage, that my friend Paula had been paying for. As I was unpacking one of the boxes, I found my <u>Sacred Path Cards</u> book. I prayed, asking for guidance and pulled the Field of Plenty card. To the best of my understanding, the Native American teachings of the Field of Plenty is about letting go of a fear of scarcity and poverty, knowing there is plenty for all. On the card is a colorful picture of a cornucopia basket full of the fresh harvest of fruits, vegetables and other produce. A reminder to be grateful now to the Creator, as if you already have it, whatever you desire, which I am ashamed to say I had forgotten in my misery, the African spirituality that the Ausar Auset Society Church had already taught me similar. Whatever you imagine and daydream about does comes true. Especially, as you put ideas that come to mind into creative problem-solving. The ability to imagine and be creative is my Het Heru destiny. How could I have forgotten?

I truly had a lot to be grateful for. My needs have been met without me purposely visualizing anything, but

I had been in too much despair and hopelessness to notice. I began expressing, aloud when I was alone in my room, my gratitude and what I wanted for my future, that I could now believe was possible. Within a month after reading the <u>Sacred Path Cards</u> book, the homeless services agency moved me to a large, one-bedroom apartment with my own kitchen, where I could cook my own food.

The I Ching had previously warned me there would be a "decrease in status but not to worry about it because later I will get what I went after." I was very grateful for the I Ching and other books given to me for a divine guidance to inspire me to keep the faith and to let me know when I am on the right path, to keep going and to persevere.

The book, <u>Light Emerging</u>, also explains about cycles as "expansion and contraction." I had two beautiful years of expansion, then later in 1998 began my contraction years. The unemployment situation made me be still, and I began to be more relaxed and be grateful for this quiet, restful period in my life, only because I intuitively know the futility and uselessness of trying to make something happen before it's time.

Chapter 8: Healing Emotionally

The other part of my career guidance reading that previously in 1991 was the Metu Neter card: Amen hetep. How was I to obtain and maintain inner peace, taking neither gain nor loss to heart when my life seemed to be full of ongoing losses and health crises? Loss of my career included.

There was plenty to be grateful for, but there were some mornings when my body was too tired and in pain to want to drag it out of bed that I felt very ungrateful for waking up in the morning. I went to the 12 step meetings to remind me to take it one day at a time, and to accept the things I cannot change, being powerless over most things and people. However, I cringed hearing people answer the greeting, "How are you?" with they were "fine because they woke up that morning." Many days I wondered why I was alive, and what my life purpose was, no longer having a clue of what my dreams and goals were.

I realized I must have been still grieving, when tears came while I walked down the street as I thought about the therapist's question, "Are you feeling better?"

I responded, "A little. I'm not feeling my best. I haven't had especially good days."

I was better than a month ago because I'm not having constant emotional pain that made me want to die. But feeling blah with no excitement or pleasure, motivation or goals is not living either. It's just going through the motions, just wanting to get the day over with.

My grieving, I imagine it's similar to withdrawal when nothing ever matches the initial euphoric high. Nothing at that moment matched or measured up to the past two years of my life when I was an active contributing member of a community full of life and love in Vermont and in Zimbabwe. At least I didn't feel empty, which was a horrible feeling I had before, worse at some times than others. It's more like feeling blah, as if something's missing.

Grieving also came in the form of an inability to accept complements because it was painful to remember when I used to change my hairstyle daily, sewed and designed my own color coordinated clothes, painted very detailed proportioned pictures, had a good memory, took good care of my health the best I knew how, was a very spiritual person, just to name a few. Other people don't seem to see this side of me, although some somehow commented, "You look like a church lady. Will you pray for me?"

Returning from Zimbabwe, it was grief on top of grief. I'd also left behind my siblings when I moved to Chicago. With health problems and no income,

I didn't know how to get back to them. I was just surviving. It was difficult to grieve the loss of my mother because I didn't know if she was alive or dead. Memories surfaced of missing my father. In therapy sessions, the counselors didn't focus on grieving they focused on past trauma.

When I became homeless, as a requirement for receiving social services for housing, the caseworkers at REST referred me to individual therapy at the Quetzal Center for sexual abuse survivors, as well as domestic violence therapy at another location, although these incidents occurred twelve years ago. I hadn't had therapy in nine years.

My therapist at the Quetzal Center was from Central America, so she understood some of my struggles. A few months after I became her patient, she went on maternity leave and transferred me to another therapist in her absence. The other therapist was an art therapist. When my regular therapist returned, they decided to ask me if I wanted to join the agency's women's art therapy group. It was great because the art therapists taught us a different watercolor technique each week. This was exciting for me because I had planned to take watercolor painting classes if I had stayed at the School of the Art Institute of Chicago. At $1400 a semester! Here the art therapists were teaching us for free.

For the new year of 2000, the art therapist gave us the assignment of making artwork relating to our personal goals and achievements from 1999, and then make a painting relating to goals for 2000. We were asked to make a group project from each of our previous paintings.

The therapist said, "See if you could see parts of each other's artwork that you could use in your individual artwork. Would you be willing to cut a piece out and give it to someone else?"

I said, "No, because I had just thought of some ideas I wanted to add to my painting from last week." I tried to suggest to her it would be better to borrow parts using a scanner to make a group project without cutting or destroying our original artwork.

The previous week, I took the risk of painting a picture of myself as a child in a dark terrifying place. But I didn't have time, plus I didn't feel safe to put in the dark silhouettes of the people who abused me surrounding me. When I looked at the picture today, I realized that I expected my family, even my siblings to protect me or at least stand up and say, "This is wrong." But all of us were in this secret grip of abuse together. The social workers stopped coming to check on us at the foster home, so no one reported the daily crazy happenings in that house. Thirty years later, I still felt the terror of being trapped with no way out.

I was outvoted, so I just went along with the art project. Seeing that others were able to give up almost all of their original work, helped me to lower my resistance. Some were very colorful designs that I thought would lose its meaning and image if it were cut apart and separated.

In the excitement of seeing the multiple possibilities of incorporating other's paintings, I actually forgot about wanting to complete my picture from last week. There was somehow power in being able to ask for artwork from others and being flattered that others made requests from me. But what was most powerful for me was observing the effect of cutting my dark ominous painting down to a manageable size and adding light and support from other's more cheerfully colored artwork. This is something I actually asked for help with last week; to visualize little Haneefa getting the help she needed and finding a safe way out, instead of withdrawal for survival.

I wondered if another woman in the group experienced similar, as she cut her brick wall of shame and silence from the past down to a smaller size. Last week, she told us the wall was too high to climb over and if she tried it would just get higher.

One of the therapist facilitators asked and suggested, "Wasn't there a faster way to get past that wall than axing it down? Wouldn't it be easier today to let others help and even share some of the load by acknowledging your wall of struggle in their own artwork?"

There were days that I felt like crying when I was out in public and on buses. Especially when I saw someone who reminded me of my friend Inviolatta who lived in Zimbabwe, and later I saw a woman who looked like Abeba from

Eritrea. They were my classmates at The School for International Training. I really missed them as friends but noticed that I cry less often. Earlier I would have had uncontrollable tears streaming down my face whenever I thought of my friends along with grieving for the life, accomplishments, and potential I had before I became ill, unemployed, homeless and deserted. Memories of the above mentioned women friends, represented the best times I had in my whole adult life.

Perhaps I was feeling less hopeless as I realized I could still accomplish some of the things I had planned to do before all of this happened. Or even start new projects with some of the education and training I've had. I just would have to pace myself. I still got frustrated with the awful constant pain in my hands and back.

Chapter 9: Spiritual Practices

In the early days of my homelessness, my friend Paula invited me to an African American Buddhist group. They met regularly in a room in a funeral home. I thought about joining the group and I really thought the decision would be an easy yes. After all, wasn't this what I've been looking for and wanted? Had I not been waiting for a group of supportive like-minded spiritual people?

But the decision was not easy. When I started coming out of the depression and being honest with myself, I really felt like running in the opposite direction, far away from it and any other spiritual groups. Some teachings I did not agree with, based on my own personal spiritual experiences, especially after having a near death experience in 1982, and with the wonderful miracles and changes in my life afterwards. It is difficult for most people who have had near death experiences to accept most religions' and organizations' teachings and frightening rules about how to relate to "God" because we've already been to heaven, and met with an incredible Light of peace, love, and acceptance. Returning to an earthly body, we develop and continue a personal relationship with God. The aftereffects of a near death experience has survivors seeing the world a completely different way. Our values change so that we are not concerned so much about material things, status, or the physical body.

This just is. It's not a virtue nor makes me special. In fact, it's like a curse in a world where greed and selfishness are the expected norm. There was no reason for me to meet in a funeral home or nearby cemeteries to release my fear of death, because I had no fear of dying. Nor how to release any attachments to possessions since I was learning daily how to live homeless, without even a dollar in my pocket.

First, of my other reasons for hesitation with joining, in addition to not wanting to have to deny my spiritual experiences, is I learned the hard way that being so self-disciplined in following religious rules was detrimental to my health, relationships and my career. My commitment was extreme in comparison to most other people who pick and choose which of the rules they wanted to follow. They couldn't seem to ever find the time to meditate, they ate what they wanted to eat. For me, this was not a conscious option. The physical changes after having a near death experience make unhealthy eating a painful experience. Many near death experiencer's acquire allergies to almost everything, including food, and their digestive systems can no longer tolerate eating meat. I can't listen to radio or watch TV for long because I, as with most near death experiences can't stand high especially loud electronic frequencies. This can make living with people, including family and friends, complicated.

When clinic lab test results showed that my red blood cells were enlarged, I went to the library to see what it meant. I was horrified to read that megaloblastic macrocytic anemia is often from vitamin B12 deficiency, which is common in people who don't eat enough meat. Meat is the main source of natural vitamin B12. You would have to do like the old Total cereal television advertisement, and eat 10 to 20 bowls of beans, nuts, greens, etc. After learning that being a strict vegan probably caused me permanent nerve damage, that could happen in as little as six months, just imagine me being vegan for ten years! I was especially reluctant to join another spiritual group that emphasized vegetarianism was the way to nirvana.

Second, the more disciplined, the more spiritual and self-help healing and character building I've done, the less friends I had. It would be nice to think of myself as a positive role model, but the truth of it is — people resent strong, assertive, honest people. I was at the stage of my spiritual growth of having to live truth daily in the moment, in spite of what others think. But people could no longer relate or understand me, and I was having a hard time relating to them or the world since being homeless and unemployed I had no active role or place in the community or society. A very lonely place to be.

In religious organizations as well as with my family and friends, I've been such a "good girl" that the religious leaders don't seem to think I needed spiritual counseling. Other members would demand all the attention and get it, along with advice, material needs and financial help. I often helped the leaders help other people while my needs were neglected. So I felt let down and reluctant to depend on spiritual leaders. Although I was in an 'abyss' as the I Ching described my situation, where I did not know which way to turn or what to do. There is a saying, the more you know — the more you realize how much you really don't know. I truly didn't know what to do, but spiritual leaders couldn't help me.

As a result of doing spiritual practices, meditations and following divine guidance, my life has taken so many detours away from the rational concept of planned goals that I stopped making long-term goals. I did make some goals of course, daily and weekly, but in life there are no guarantees. From this perspective I wasn't usually shattered when plans didn't work out — until now.

Much of my fear of joining a new African American Buddhist group, was of my fear of being alone again, even within an organization. The worst feeling is to be alone in a crowd. If I'm going to be alone, I might as well be alone of my own choosing. Same with in my marriages, my spouses were out drinking, drugging, and partying. My husband put me on a pedestal as if I were a saint, while he was out doing his thing. I was at home alone unless I wanted to join him. Partying is boring as hell to me. Everyone looks like they're enjoying themselves except me, while I'm miserable because I can't relate to them and they can't relate to me. To me, nights are for sleeping and there is only trouble in the streets at night. When we were at home together there was little to talk about. I couldn't understand his need for the street life. He couldn't understand me. With my abusive second husband, I did not even try to understand him.

Third, I was done with male authoritarian religion leaders,

especially when they criticize other religion's beliefs and practices while preaching that their way is the only way. For example, that the way I learned to meditate was wrong. He told us that it was a form of dreaming, of sleep. Never mind how much the deep breathing, music and visualizations had healed me, because he didn't give me the opportunity to tell him. By then, I had heard similar from people who had tried holotropic breathwork and not seen their past lives, and therefore said I must have dreamed what I saw. How do men get to be spiritual leaders since men have a tougher time going into deep meditation and trance, tending to intellectualize in books and lectures about what they wished were their own mystical spiritual experiences?

I had to admit to myself my strong inner desire is to live a full life, which would include family, friends, and a community. This was painful to admit to myself after knowing what it was like to always be surrounded by caring people in Zimbabwe. The village families never left me alone not even in my bed at night. Now that I was back in the United States, it seemed cruel to give someone something they have always wanted and more, and then take it away. Not some of it but it seemed like all of it! Is my life lesson to test how much that I would I allow myself to revert back to my habitual defense mechanism of the lonely child personality?

From this life lesson, in a short amount of time as I was given the opportunity to go through what very poor and possibly homeless people go through of gaining humility from experiencing discrimination, abuse, and injustices.

One person told me, "You can learn a lot from homeless people. They have no shame." I was beginning to understand why. There's a certain freedom to being an outcast from society, similar to freedom as a visitor in Africa or any foreign culture or country. Everything is so radically different from all that you've been taught to believe. It kind of forces you to give up your old beliefs and prioritize what's most important in life.

Initially, being homeless was very confusing and terrifying but it offered a liberating growing experience. Hopefully this is just a healing interval, and I will have even better relationships where there is a balance of me equally sharing and receiving unconditional love. From in the mist of my emotional, pain I can better understand other people's pain and why they do and say the things they do and be compassionate. Perhaps later I would be able to help them acknowledge and heal the source of their pain too.

PART TWO: Is There a Home for Me?

Chapter 10: A Push Out the Door

My aunt had been asking me to move out to the suburbs with her for the past few months. Her son moved out and she didn't want to live alone. I've been hesitating because I wanted my independence. I was still hoping to have doctors fix me so that I could be employed. Plus I knew from visiting her in the suburbs, that the buses run slow, at half hour to an hour intervals, and rarely or not at all on the weekends.

Moving in with my Aunt? I Ching Hexagram 26 (lines 4 and 6) into Hexagram 34. Metu Neter cards: Nekebet tu tchaas/Geb hetep.

I Ching Hexagram 26 is again about "crossing the water" meaning traveling beyond your home territory and usual circle of friends, family and acquaintances. Line 4: don't wait until situation is too far along and causes harm. Line 6: the time for obstructions has passed therefore success. Hexagram 34 is about perseverance as the way opens up with less resistance. Warned not to force the situation, nor be overconfident. Further, what was very true in my case, was the encouragement to give up my defensiveness and insecurity since I would be going to an environmental that would not be threatening.

Transitional housing for the homeless still meant wandering from place to place. From one room with a shared bathroom, to a nice quiet one bedroom apartment, to being squeezed into a small studio apartment. The landlords could throw us all out again at any time. How much worse could it get?

One night, I woke to the sound of paper rustling and crunch, crunch. My ears perked up while I looked around the dark room. I didn't see anyone. Sounded like it was coming from the small bookshelf where I stored food near the kitchen, since there was only a couple of cabinets above the sink. Otherwise, the kitchen was simply a stove and refrigerator on one wall. It quieted, and I slept.

In the morning I found holes in bags of rice, my gluten-free flours and small boxes on the shelf. This reminded me of when I was a teenager, we woke to find on the kitchen table, a long round tunnel eaten out, through the middle, from one end of the long loaf of bread to the other, by mice.

However, after I put my non-perishable food in more secure containers on the bookshelf, the noises continued at night. I heard cans and boxes being knocked off the shelf, but I didn't hear squeaks. It would have had to be several mice together to be able to push those big items onto the floor. Now I was really scared because it couldn't possibly be mice! Did someone's pet hamster get loose?

Timidly, I reached for the flashlight by my bedside. Staying in bed, I peer into the darkness. It's huge. It's gray and menacing as it darted away. My can of cashews is on the floor. Seems to like sweets, not the plain instant oatmeal but my apple cinnamon, and chewed through my Raisin Crisp cereal box.

Terrified to go to sleep at night. The shelf was to the left of the foot of my bed. Could it be a rat? When I was younger, I had heard stories of babies in cribs getting bit by rats. Now in my one room, small studio apartment there was nowhere for me to run. Whatever it was, was bold because I couldn't scare it away by yelling and making my own loud noises,

"Go away! I want to sleep!" Several minutes later, I would hear it chewing again. Maybe he was in the garbage or behind the cabinet or there could be others underneath my bed. What if it got on my bed with me!

The janitor and management at the apartment building didn't want to believe it could be a rat, insisting it was a mouse. All I knew was that that tiny studio apartment wasn't big enough fo the two of us. So my friend James brought a huge rat trap, smeared the middle with peanut butter, and set the trap. He put poison out and told me to cover the drains in the kitchen sink, make sure the sink was dry at night and close the lid on the toilet.

A couple of days later, the rat decided to eat the peanut butter and got caught. He was shockingly longer than the rat trap! I took pictures with my camera. Now we had proof.

My apartment was on the first floor across from the back door. More than the rat was a menace. Drug addicts and drug dealers living in the building kept up loud music, partying and arguments in the stairwell and hallways at night.

The rat was the last straw. Although James nailed on a metal draft stopper to close the big gap in the bottom of the door, it was past time for me to make a move. Heaven has a way of giving us all a push. A frightening push out the door. Forcing us to take that step forward and close the old doors behind us.

Chapter 11: Family

I moved in with Aunt Gussie. There were power struggles between us in the beginning. My uncle explained to me that the situation was similar to him living in a rooming house sharing a bathroom and kitchen with others. The landlord was the boss. This was difficult for me to accept because I was paying rent. Most of my life I worked and paid rent, even paid the rent when I had husbands. So I was expecting more independence. In time I calmed down, took it in stride, and gained more respect from my aunt.

From my experience and observation, when people move in with each other, as the honeymoon phase quickly fades away, the first year is going to be naturally rough with power struggles of "Why are you telling me what to do?" With time you begin to trust, learn how to lean on each other, and to appreciate each other. Knowing that this will happen, may help save many relationships whether roommates, or family members, or romantic relationships. It helped me cooperate more with my aunt.

My siblings and their children and grandchildren came to Aunt Gussie's house when Mother Dear came to visit, uniting the family. What's best about living with Aunt Gussie, is she connected me to the elder members of my family. I was getting to know her, cousins, my other great uncles and aunts for the first time. They came into town and stayed at Aunt Gussie's house for about a week or a weekend to go to visit their sister Dorothy and brother Roy in a nursing home. My paternal grandmother, Mother Dear was in her 90s at the time, smart and spry. Her brothers were ten and twelve years younger. It was difficult for me to keep from laughing as they argued, about which one of them couldn't tell them what to do. My grandmother being the oldest was of course bossing them which they didn't like, and because she was older they would try to take care of her which she didn't want because she was still quite independent.

I loved hearing them tell stories about their childhood, parents, what it was like to be back in their hometown compared to when they were younger, about historical events like the Depression and blizzards, and before there were modern conveniences. Going way back in history, considering Mother Dear was 92 years old at the time of this telling, and she was born in 1911. The following history is from audio recordings, transcriptions, and notes from Uncle Dennis, Uncle Pete and Machilla sitting around talking at Aunt Gussie's kitchen table.

Mother Dear: "My maternal grandparents were from St. Louis. Mother Dear's mother's mother was married to the son of the slave owner. She had eighteen children. The first two were by the slave owner and the other sixteen were by his son. Like his father, he was very mean. He used to take his wife out to the woods regularly to beat her. One day, she followed him submissively to the woods for her beating. Sarah, his sister said, "I'm going too." When they got to the woods, she pulled out a pistol pointed it at him, and told him, "Now you try to beat her." He never beat his wife ever again. She left him though, because he still was so mean. She took seven of her children and left him. She came to Illinois and he went to Oklahoma. Our mother's father had a lot of land in Oklahoma. He was very ambitious. When he died, his land was divided up among his ten children.

The first house Mother Dear remembers, was near the railroad tracks in the suburb where Aunt Gussie lives now. After awhile, they moved to a nearby suburb that had mostly Italians, who could be mean, but were good to our family. A large family with twelve children. Two siblings died young.

Dennis: "When we talk about family members, I give some credence to the fact that there were twelve of us children. But in actuality, I talk about only ten because I didn't know the other two. I didn't know Agnes and I didn't know Douglas."

Mother Dear: "Douglas died when he was 11 months old, of pneumonia. I was two years old, and I remember going to the funeral. Agnes was thirteen years old when she got burned. She got burned terrible, to the point where her mouth was even crisp. Our mother told us she didn't even know how Agnes could even talk, but she did tell us how she got burned. She was trying to light a coal stove. She put the kerosene on the coals in the stove, and lit the match, but the coals didn't light. She came back to it, but because combustion had built up inside the stove, it flared up setting her long pretty hair on fire and burning her face. She could barely talk in the hospital because she just had a small opening for a mouth. She lived seven hours.

They had this black undertaker, Jones, in Chicago. Mama and them, didn't know then that he had the reputation of being a swindler. When we were in the church getting ready for the funeral, there was a mouse squeaking in the casket! You could hear it squeaking and running around throughout the casket. When the funeral was over and we went to the cemetery, the undertaker was supposed to have the grave ready right? Well, Agnes couldn't be buried because there was no grave dug. So, they put her in the mausoleum and told us to come back tomorrow. Mama and some friends went back the next day and the undertaker didn't even show up. The body was supposed to be in the mausoleum. Later Mama started getting all this information from people that he was a swindler anyway. So, to this day we don't know whatever happened to Agnes's body. It couldn't have been in that casket! We all said it, because the casket couldn't be open anyway. We should have figured that when we heard the mouse squeaking and when we went to the cemetery that was just a formality. He was just trying to fool somebody. Mama had given him the down payment, but they decided to not finish paying him anymore because they couldn't get Agnes buried. Some neighbors were saying Mama sold the body because Agnes had this unusual ailment, a deformity of the inside of her body. Agnes was home from school that day, because she had a medical condition that caused her to pass out, anywhere. The cause according to the doctor was that she had a uterus and vagina that lacked a "sieve." Previously there were plans made to have an operation. It could be that the doctors got together with the undertaker to get that body part.

I remember going to the funeral. I was six years old, sitting up there. I remember looking at my father with tears dropping down his eyes. Like drops of water, the tears were just that big! He loved his Agnes. Ummm hummmm. That was his joy. She was very nice looking as I remember. She had thick hair. Long thick hair down her back. It was his first daughter. It upset Mama for about a year. I don't know how she kept it together.

Let's talk about another subject. Papa couldn't carry a note as far as singing is concerned, and yet he had a brother who could really sing. Oscar was something else."

Pete: "You said Papa couldn't sing a note. Somewhere, somebody told me that Papa had a beautiful voice and sang in a couple of church choirs."

Mother Dear: "Papa did sing in the church choir. But a lot of people singing church choirs but that doesn't mean they have a beautiful voice. You are right about him singing in the choir."

Pete: Only thing I know about Oscar, and it stuck in my mind because Mama made a comment one time, "The only time we see these people is when they are broke and they come looking for money."

Mother Dear: "I don't know why they were like that! Even Willie Mae. You were too young to know her. She got married, she and her husband would come out and Papa had to give them carfare back home. I don't know why they thought Papa and Mama had so much money. She never came up without Papa giving her carfare back home. That was his sister, and he loved that sister too.

Well, let me get back to explaining to you what I was hoping you'd understand last night. When I was growing up, the piano had seven keys in the middle and has seven keys in other different sections. The seven keys were do, ray, me, fa, so, la, ti, do. Over the years it changed and now it's C, D, E, F, G, A, B, and C. When I had a piano teacher, she never went into that. I didn't know "do," from whatever. I didn't know the names of the keys. I don't know what was wrong with me. Miss Courtney told Mama that I couldn't come anymore. How come I couldn't come? She didn't teach me how. But when I look back over that situation, I could have had a piano teacher if she had taught me. But she shouldn't have said I couldn't come back. She probably did it because she thought I could hear, and I could hear. I was playing the notes right. But I didn't know what the notes were. Later, I did do piano recitals and drawing. Recently, I returned to playing the piano, and I am learning to play the hymns for the Jehovah Witness Hall.

Pete: Let me tell you something. When I was in college, I had some room for some electives, so I took a piano class. After about three months the teacher said to me, "Why did you take this class?" I never practiced. I didn't do nothing. She gave me assignments and I'd get up the morning before class and try to do it. So when she said to me, 'Why did you take this class?' I said to her, 'Ma'am, have no fear. I'll make sure I won't take it again.'

Life is interesting though when you look back over it. I look back at my life and I think, 'Boy, if Mama had known what I was doing, she would have killed me herself. I deserved all the 500 whippings that I got as a child. Teachers used to ask me if I was holding up the family reputation of my older brothers Dennis and Robert.

Mama would send us out to chose our own switch. I tried choosing a switch that I knew would break. She would make me go get another one. Sometimes she would beat us naked, without our clothes on with an ironing cord. Sometimes, I would hide under the bed. Papa didn't like discipling us children and would only whip us if he was pressured by Mama. Most of the time Papa would just tell us to hold out our hand and he would hit it with a pencil. But there were times to be honest when he would beat our behinds.

Our sister Dorothy was so full of life. That girl sure could dance, she could roller skate too, and rode bicycles, and I don't know what else. Nothing seems to bother her. She has a good memory of family history and events. Dorothy also has a beautiful smile, and sense of humor that keeps us laughing. (Too bad she had the stroke).

I was also a good dancer. We used to "cut the rug" at the dance hall before it became Rock of Ages Church. Mama used to come and watch us young people dance.

I worked 17 years as a caseworker at a public assistance office. I tried having my own fish market, but it only lasted a year. As the youngest sibling, and the youngest boy, I had to learn to fight. I started out in life fighting more than I would have liked. I served in World War II. Was a secretary at the Veteran's Administration. Now I have three grown children. After retirement, I drove a school bus for awhile."

***

On one of the visits, Mother Dear and Aunt Gussie baked a sweet potato pie together. It was fun to watch them combine ideas for spices and other ingredients. Aunt Gussie was known as quite a baker of southern fried apple pies and assorted cakes whose names I had not heard of before.

James came a long way on buses and trains to visit me at Aunt Gussie's home. My family welcomed him in. One time he came through a blizzard to visit me. I was truly heartfelt touched that he would care that much for me. Of course I fussed at him, worried about his safety. When James didn't come for several months, my great aunts and uncles got in the car and took me to my old neighborhood on the north side of Chicago to look for James.

By the end of the year, Aunt Gussie began to trust and confide in me. She asked me questions about life and the afterlife as she talked about how much she missed her husband. He came to her in her dreams and was letting her know of his spirit presence by interfering with her radio and occasionally playing their favorite songs. She frequently asked me if these occurrences were real. Aunt Gussie worried about past situations where she had lingering guilt and regrets. Our discussions helped ease her concerns.

Chapter 12: Not Again!

Aunt Gussie taught me a lot about communication. How to talk to people. She would repeat what she said to me until I answered with real interest, with creativity instead of just nodding. Most importantly, she taught me how to listen. To really listen to what people are saying, not just with what I'm hearing with my ears but what they are say with their hearts. To go beyond words to their intention in spite of accidentally saying it wrong. Whether when only saying a few words, or going on and on and on. I learned to appreciate each person for being. Aunt

Gussie also taught my ears to hear better by her talking to me from the other end of her house. I'm not sure how this was possible since I had been hard of hearing since I was twenty five years old. She herself had remarkable hearing. She could hear my soft voice from the kitchen to the living room.

I observed how she was with her friends. She listened to her family and friends any time of night or day. And I saw how her friends are friends of each other with patience and compassion. Through her stubbornness, Aunt Gussie taught me to speak up for myself and others. Together we taught each other it was okay to say our true feelings and fears. The true meaning of what it means to be strong.

I did not know then that these conversations with my aunt foretold what was coming next. She got shingles for which medicine didn't relieve the pain. Several months later, she began complaining of an awful pain in her upper leg. However, this did not stop her from doing household chores or going out with friends. Aunt Gussie increasingly spent more time sitting on the living room couch. Her doctor ordered an MRI scan but her leg was too painful for her to lie still long enough. The clinic told her to get more pain medicine from her doctor and schedule another appointment. Unfortunately, before my aunt could go for the MRI, she had a minor stroke. After admission to the hospital they did tests and were planning to do surgery on her hip. During the surgery they discovered that there was nothing to attach a hip replacement to, because cancer had destroyed the bone in her leg. The doctors told Aunt Gussie that she had six weeks to live.

Her daughters had difficulty coping. They argued. One daughter angrily banned friends and the rest of the family from visiting their mother in the hospital and later at her home. They tried to put me out and I had to scramble to find affordable housing. At such short notice, it was not possible because most affordable housing have years-long waiting lists. I could no longer climb stairs even with help, my legs would feel like wet spaghetti and would go out from under me without warning. When I walked too far, I had severe back pain afterwards especially at night. Eventually, I had to use a wheelchair and needed to find accessible housing.

Mother Dear came with a friend and drove me around to apply for apartments and to social service agencies. Uncle Dennis also came to help. All the affordable accessible apartments had long waiting lists.

Chapter 13: Sacred Contracts Archetypes Cards

In 2002, while I was living with Aunt Gussie, I discovered the book, <u>Sacred Contracts: Awakening Your Divine Potential</u>. Curious about archetypes I wanted to see how they related to the West African Yoruba deities' descriptions of human personality characteristics and abilities. The author, Caroline Myss, explains that your initial Archetypal Wheel is similar to a astrology birth chart so you only make an Archetypal Wheel once. Later when you inquire about a situation, you will use these same twelve archetype cards. Following the instructions in the book for choosing my personal archetypes, I first thought of a few roles that I have been most of my life, such as being a natural teacher, artist, nurse, and speaking up for justice. Then I read and chose other archetypes from the descriptions in the Gallery of Archetypes in the appendix in the back of the book. Each archetype represents learning experiences, and with recognition of our own main archetypal patterns, can help guide us through life. There is also an [Archetype Card](#) deck available with 74 archetypes by Caroline Myss, but her book, Sacred Contracts gives more in-depth descriptions than the cards.

Each archetype, such as the Artist, has several different aspects to help narrow down whether the archetype accurately describes you or not.

To assemble my Chart of Origin (Archetypal Wheel) I deep breathed, did the meditative visualization for opening to intuitive guidance, next with my eyes closed I followed the instructions to pair each of my chosen archetypes with shuffled stack of twelve numbers to represent the twelve traditional astrology houses.

Later, I started answering the long list of questions in the book for the first two archetypes that I chose but stopped because being analytical contradicts being able to be intuitive. Being too much in one's head thinking, questioning and judging prevents connecting to one's true Self and intuitive spirit guidance.

My Chart of Origin (Archetypal Wheel):

First House: Ego Personality: Amateur

Second House: Life Values: Judge

Third House: Self-Expression Siblings: Saboteur

Fourth House: Home: Prostitute

Fifth House: Creativity Good Fortune: Wounded Healer

Sixth House: Occupation Health: Wounded/Nature Child

Seventh House: Marriage Relationship: Slave

Eighth House: Other Peoples Resources: Hermit

Ninth House: Spirituality: Addict

Tenth House: Highest Potential: Victim

Eleventh House: Relationship to The World: Rescuer

Twelfth House: The Unconscious: Artist

Reasons Why I Choose These Archetypes

First House: Ego Personality: Amateur. It's true that I have many varied talents and abilities, do well with each but am somewhat a "master of none." I developed many of my talents but as the definition of "amateur" indicates, I've rarely marketed my talents nor sold what I created. Most of my creations are artistic. Some people consider art a hobby instead of a profession, probably because of low wages and inconsistent opportunities. Self-taught, I don't have college degrees in art, but I have perfected crafts, fine arts such as drawing and painting, writing, baking, sewing, knitting, also designing and sewing clothing and home furnishings. With a good memory, intuition, teaching, research and analytical abilities I might make much more income off of counseling or being an administrative assistant.

During my childhood my mother nurtured my artistic abilities. Then at age eight, all of this attention stopped when she married my stepfather. Later my foster parents criticized yet sold my artwork at art fairs, without sharing the profits with me. They criticized most everything about us children. Made me hate and not trust compliments because our talents were also exploited in other ways. Like telling me I did such a wonderful job at shining pots and pans then assigned me the daily task of washing pots in addition to my other household chores. Initially I actually did like shining pots and pans! This knocked down my confidence and later made me fearful of more exploitation if I were to sell my artwork myself.

Conversely, the ability to create was the only power and control I had in the abusive foster home. As an adult, I could give my all, while caring for patients and students in spite of bureaucracy and discrimination, as long as I had creative time at home. So I would get up early in the morning and do art or sewing before I went to work at 7:30 AM. My individual power to create that I did not have to fight over with anyone. It was mine alone. No need to conform in order to make it marketable. This gave me freedom to create, gain confidence and take risks. My connection to the divine. Remaining an amateur artist was the one area of my life where I didn't have to be competitive. The trade-off, of course is that I could have had more financial stability if I had risked selling my talents and been more willing to climb the professional career ladder. I also could've been more connected to family, community, and society instead of the many hours spent in creative solitude.

I had to quit going to the famous School of the Art School of Chicago after only one year because I was becoming literally an "starving artist." Although I had partial scholarships and loans, unlike other college majors where students buy their textbooks at the beginning of this semester and they're done, in art school teachers would require us, at least twice a week to buy and try out different kinds of paper, paints, pencils and brushes. Large sheets of tinted or textured drawing and watercolor papers were expensive. I had to decide whether to buy art supplies or groceries.

Second House: Life Values: Judge.
I originally considered the Judge archetype because of its shadow characteristic of harsh criticism without compassion. I chose the Judge as an afterthought, because I thought I was supposed to choose 12 archetypes. I didn't know that I was to only choose eight archetypes, until I saw

the instructions were that everyone already has the four primary survival archetypes of the Prostitute, Saboteur, Victim, and Child. I groaned when I scrambled my chosen archetypes and pulled the Judge card! But as I reread the description of the Judge, I began to see more of the positives in my character. I have been a natural mediator most of my life as a second-born middle child, the peacemaker in my marriages and at events. I try to get both sides to be seen, heard and understood. While at the School for International Training in 1997, I enjoyed the Peace and Conflict, and Mediation classes and activities. We role-played mediating the Arab and Israel conflict as well as the then Yugoslavia (now Bosnia) conflict. It was difficult work because there's usually someone leading that wants to stay angry, revengeful, stepping on other people in order to maintain power. People follow them out of fear, and the more the possibility of the truth coming out, the more threatening the leader becomes. But the citizens, especially the youth who don't understand why they should be enemies have been coming together to get to know each other, for peace.

The Judge is appropriate to the second house because the second house represents life values and use of physical power. I could've gone either way with my upbringing, surrounded by lack of justice and compassion choosing to be either like my parental role models as a way to survive, or choose to have my own values and morals. I chose the latter. It has felt like hell and was very lonely, but I stuck with my values even when life got rough. In my marriage, I got tired of being placed on a pedestal, while the husband went out and did his dirt and then came home criticizing me to no end. Expecting me to be superhuman and to just put up with his behavior and lack of responsibility.

My struggles with power were mostly about values. During my younger years, I was overpowered by others who believed just taking what they wanted was just a way of life. Many times, I did without physical needs if it meant lying, stealing, or being cruel in order to get it. Or having to fight with other people. I came to believe either you want to give it to me – or you don't! I wasted a lot of years and time waiting for "loved ones" or jobs to do the right thing. After all, weren't they supposed to?

Then I discovered good people in the world and connection to the universe. Complete strangers would walk up to me and give me what I needed. Teaching me that I am divinely blessed with all that I need. Somehow my silent thoughts and wants were heard. I learned not to fear men and not to depend on them for my needs, instead of what I was previously taught from childhood to believe.

In regards to the shadow side of the Judge, I used to be critical of others because I used to be very critical of myself. As I became more forgiving and compassionate with myself, I was gradually able to do the same with others. Also I had somewhat of a unconscious "superiority complex" which is funny because my mother used to tell me I had an "inferiority complex" when I was a young child. Of course, I had no idea what she meant. Within a few years I did acquire an inferiority complex because my stepfather and foster father criticized almost everything about me. Almost everything we children did was wrong. Accordingly, as an adult some of my being judgmental was a defense mechanism to protect me from allowing others to treat me that way. It wasn't until at age thirty-five, when an elder asked me, "Why do you try to be better than other people," that I realized I have been so focused on 'trying to catch up with my peers' thinking that they knew more than I did and had more experience, that I didn't realize that I actually excelled in many areas.

Third House: Self-Expression Siblings: Saboteur. The saboteur landed in my third house and this makes sense in terms of my being able to express myself. When I was younger, I was so shy I didn't say much of anything, as a result, I was the only one of my siblings the judge ordered to have psychotherapy, labeling me as "socially retarded." I would be so self-conscious I'd choose my few words very carefully. In later years health problems caused me to speak too slow and too soft and often the wrong words came out. People did not have the patience to hear me out. However, not able to tolerate injustices, people were shocked when I did speak up, in defense of others. Then my mouth got me in trouble!

Prior to the years of 1999-2002 when I first became physically disabled, I didn't believe that I could ask for what I needed and receive it. Or that people even cared enough to listen to what I said, so this habit was probably also an unconscious reason for my soft voice. People had to lean in closer to hear me. However, becoming physically disabled forced me to become angry enough to fight for my rights and to become appropriately assertive.

It was also in midlife that I became aware of the consequences of having negative thoughts. For me, it wasn't so much being angry or resentful towards other people, as it was that I was pessimistic about wanting anything out of life. Therefore, I stopped getting much out of my life. By then I was afraid that other people would steal whatever I had. I'd expect the worst, since life was one crisis after another, after another. I also would leave situations prematurely because of perceived hurts. In these ways, I sabotaged myself.

Change is uncomfortable, especially with the fear of the unknown. But I don't think I really had the luxury of resisting change. I've left abusive relationships and jobs much more than other people would have. Surrounded by people who stayed in abusive situations for 15, 20 years or more, I felt ashamed and isolated. Often embarrassed because I neither lived in one place or worked at the same job for more than four years. I also followed my intuition and took the risks of going to other states to college, and even to other countries. My siblings have always lived in the same city where we grew up. Now I know moving on is healthy.

Fourth House: Home: Prostitute. Having a home has always been dear to me. So it makes sense home would be the area of my life where I might prostitute myself. Home is where I can feel safe enough to be myself, and to express my passions and creativity. It is where I spend most of my time and therefore will now come out fighting anyone who wants to make my home "their home." I've tried making my home with other people including my first and second husbands and it hasn't worked out well.

In many ways I did not have a home as a child. As a young child, my family moved back-and-forth to my Grandmother's house which I considered home. After age seven, I moved to different houses none of which felt like "home" because of the chaos that resided there. In addition, I was taken from my mother and put in the foster home at age 13. Somewhat my marriages were just as chaotic. I did make my apartments in adulthood "home" in terms of buying the furnishings, decorations, paying the rent, and the time I spent there in solitude doing artwork. The prostitute showed up in my life whenever I am a people pleaser, saying 'Yes' when I should say, 'No.'

It is interesting that my foster parents wouldn't let us girls go to college, and "didn't want us to work" because then we would be "prostituting ourselves." Yet, they were the ones who could have turned me into a possible prostitute in the first place by making me do sexual favors for him. In addition to having me clean up after them and their children. My people pleasing behavior carried over to my bad marriages and miserable jobs. After a while I wanted <u>home</u> more than I wanted the husband or the marriage! My second husband's wife before me, told me she actually had to act like a street prostitute to make him leave her alone.

Determined to have my own roof over my head, the jobs I had were very labor-intensive with low wages, but it allowed me to pay my rent, bills, feed and clothe myself. I'd never had a sit-down job. Up on my feet for long overtime shifts, with heavy lifting. Working gave me some "status" in the community especially since I had an education. I honestly believed that the more I gave, and accepted the poor working conditions without complaining, the more I would be respected and the more I would earn. All of which was not true. Many years of this lifestyle did eventually lead to depression and melancholy while wondering why these work ethic strategies weren't working out.

My devotion to religious organizations was probably a different way that I prostituted myself. I had a full-time job yet I was volunteering long hours, and giving my money away because I was getting some spiritual support. I sacrificed my career, financial stability and my health. After I started losing my health, I began putting my foot down and setting up limits, but by then it was too late.

Fifth House: Creativity Good Fortune: Wounded Healer. Originally chose the Healer and the Wounded Healer because I have experiences with both. I am a registered nurse, but I also inspire others to heal by encouraging them to make necessary lifestyle changes. I role-model these changes and benefits. I'm also an energy healer using reiki and prayers. The reason why I chose the Wounded Healer initially is because doctors diagnosed me with a neuromuscular disease for which there is no treatment. Therefore I would have to cure myself. Since 1988, when I read Bernie Siegel's book, <u>Love Medicine and Miracles</u>, ten years before I became ill, I've believed that personal transformation would heal me emotionally, physically and spiritually. Siegel's research and theories were based on patients with cancer. At that time, and to the present I don't have cancer. But I realized back then, that the way I was living my life would make me a prime candidate for developing cancer. So, to the best of my ability I remind myself daily to live life to the fullest, to give my body a live message.

An energy healer told me, "Physically, I didn't see a serious illness, instead your problem is mostly spiritual energy depletion. This is because you are like a sponge taking in other's negative energy. Further, it would be better for you to move away from large cities for that reason."

Soon after, I unexpectedly moved to live with my aunt in a small suburban city with single family homes.

Sixth House: Occupation Health: Wounded or Nature Child. The Wounded Child archetype of course fits for me as a survivor of childhood abuse and trauma. This is how I learned to people please, be an overachiever and perfectionist while being taken advantage of on jobs. Childhood abuse numbed me so that I functioned like a zombie. No one could really hurt me anymore because I grew a tough shell. However, I wasn't living either. In regards to occupational health, employers often called me on my days off because they could count on me to say yes. I worked long shifts without ever taking a break for a drink of water, snacks, or meals, or even to urinate. So dedicated to the patients. This continued until one day after working eleven days straight, as a nurses' aide, I was too tired to get out of bed that morning. Finally calling in sick, the supervisor gave me two weeks to rest. At the end of those two weeks, I questioned what I was allowing to be done to myself, and I quit that job.

Graduating from nursing school, my first job was as a registered nurse at a nursing home. One of my doctors suggested I apply there. The nursing home administrator hired me off the street with only a week's orientation and training. Besides having to do medication and treatments for an entire wing, later they gave me the responsibilities of supervising not just the nursing staff but for whatever happened in the whole building, along with doing treatments for patients in the rest of the building that only a registered nurse could do. Increasingly, I worked over twelve hours a day because the second shift nurse, if there was ever such a person, made a habit of calling in sick or was late. The administration informed me that I could not leave at the end of my usual eight hours because there had to be a registered nurse in the building at all times. It got to the point where I was too tired to even spend "all" the money I was making. When I had weekends off, I would go to the store but found myself wandering in circles forgetting what I came to buy. Usually I had a good memory. Previously writing a grocery list or making a mental note of what I wanted to buy, was enough to recall later.

Thereafter, I worked night shift as a registered nurse. Working nights was also not good for my health, because I couldn't sleep during the day. When the sun was up I was wide awake, even though I closed the drapes and unplugged the phone and went to bed.

I also chose the Nature Child in addition to the Wounded Child because of wild animals' relationship with me, although I've not had animals as pets at home. Growing up, other family members had pets. After my near death experience as an adult, animals appeared and communicated with me as if I understood them. They are comforting and literally lifesavers for me during stressful times. I like animals but I prefer them not caged up. Loving nature came from my childhood memories of being allowed to play in the rain and going to parks. Cities can occasionally feel like concrete prisons to me. My best health, emotionally and physically, was when I lived five months in rural areas of Zimbabwe.

Seventh House: Marriage Relationship: Slave. Every time I had to say the word "slave" while reading aloud the book, Sacred Contract's description of the Slave, I got a sick feeling in my gut. This is partly because I am of African American descent but also in my marriages I was treated as a slave. I could say similar for jobs. Except for with my second marriage, people didn't boss me around. Instead they manipulated me by abusing my kindness and naiveness. They saw that I was hard-working. Some of it probably originated from my Wounded Child background that prepped me to be a voluntary slave. My father figures only gave orders and punishment. We weren't treated as human beings. They used to tell us, "You don't think. We think for you." Initially, I put the Slave as one of my shadow archetypes.

As I explained earlier, I mistakenly chose 12 archetypes because I didn't know the instructions were to include the four primary archetypes common to everyone. When it came time to make my Archetype Wheel, I had sixteen archetypes. That meant four archetype cards I had to discard. Since I had to shuffle them anyway and lined them up with the twelve numbered cards, I just let intuition guide me to which of the remaining archetypes did belong to me. I was surprised of course, but in some ways, I should not have been surprised considering the American legacy of slavery and discrimination. After all, women are still treated as slaves at home and especially in stereotypical women's jobs. Paid low wages and expected to put up with terrible working conditions. Then go home and work another shift of housework, caregiving, compassion, romance, and pretend to be sexually aroused in marriages. These are difficult roles to get out of. There is a lot of negative societal pressure to keep us in our places. As a teenager, I decided I would work when I grew up and married, we would split the bills so he paid half and I paid half, then have my own bank account because I didn't want to be trapped into abusive marriages like my mothers were because they didn't work! Women's lib didn't tell us that bucking traditional gender family roles for women meant that if I worked, I would become the sole provider for each marriage!

Even when Black African Americans are college educated, they are still given the labor intensive jobs. For example, the Black African American nurses that graduated with me told me that when they went to interviews, although there were long columns of nursing jobs advertised in the newspaper for each hospital. Yet, they were told that there were only openings for a couple of the listings. These were geriatrics and orthopedics positions which require a lot of lifting and cleaning of incontinent patients. Jobs that no one likes to do. I experienced similar, but I assumed that I was an isolated case since I dressed as a Muslim woman back then.

Eighth House: Other People's Resources: Hermit (Mystic). I originally chose the Hermit because of my lifetime pattern of forced isolation and voluntary solitude for creative and spiritual pursuits. Isolation started with my premature birth, childhood years of abusive possessive step and foster families, a second husband and later a later physical disability. The Hermit or Mystic was not one of my first choices after reading the description of the Mystic. Forewarned that the life of a Mystic is not glamorous and instead experiences great physical and spiritual suffering, hard work, and mundane activities. Would I be ready to pay the price in blood, sweat, and tears? I have had plenty of experiences with blood, sweat and tears. Sometimes I feel like I'd gladly give both the Hermit and the Wounded Healer archetypes back! Yet, I do take comfort in spirituality and solitude. There is, however, a fine line between a healthy dose of solitude and isolation for me. The shadow side of the Hermitage is a lifetime pattern of isolation.

My first impression when I looked at my archetype wheel chart and saw the Hermit in my Eighth House: Other People's Resources was that it wasn't true for me as a Hermit. I rarely used other people's resources. I just became other people's resources! I hated money and the excuses people made to do wrong whether they have too little or too much money. Probably from my ancient ancestral biological memory, Native American and African heritage, I prefer self-sufficiency in rural surroundings although I was born in and grew up in cities and so did my parents. I sewed my husband's and my own clothes, cooked from scratch and made my own home furnishings. My siblings competed with each other trying to keep up with the Joneses. I was more practical with my dress, home and lifestyle. Borrowing was rare for me. If I could not provide my own means I simply did without. Doing without for most of my adult life. Too independent for my own good. I'm just now learning how to receive from others. Trying it out.

Family inheritance? Well, my parents didn't leave us much to inherit. What little there was from my father, my siblings argued and fought over. I wasn't even going to go to my father's funeral, but my grandmother asked me to come as a "mediator." I thought she meant assisting the family in grieving — not to be a referee! I was shocked. A few personal items given to me, and a couple items that I chose like my father's eyeglasses and a red sweater were enough for me.

As far as financial and legal matters though, I wasn't a very ambitious person. I was ambitious in terms of obtaining other goals and an education, but I wasn't a financial planner. I didn't set out planning to make so many dollars in so many years. I didn't even concentrate on the fact that an education such as nursing would pay me more money than working as a nurses' aide, I only knew that I wanted to be a nurse. And later, when I went back to college, I didn't know that I would be risking no income at all. I wasn't thinking about the consequences of school loans and being away traveling. Perhaps I didn't know, mostly because money and what I needed has always been divinely provided to me, and also because I have worked so hard previously at everything for most of my life. When I went back for my master's degree, I wasn't thinking about salaries, as much as, I knew with my failing health that I needed a sit-down job for once in my life.

Don't get me wrong, other than long-term planning such as a retirement plan, I was very financially responsible. Major credit cards were denied because I paid off my monthly balances before the interest accrued. Why should I pay interest if I didn't have to? I paid my rent and utility bills on time. I had a savings account. I split my paychecks to pay bills, with the remainder some went to savings, and some to spend. My financial future was destroyed because I let unscrupulous people take my money and possessions. As a result, I was always starting over and not getting ahead. I let other's need for money, sex, and power – overpower me. I did hire a lawyer for my first divorce which was a good strategy because later his lawyer advised my husband to sue me for spousal support!

Another reason for less socialization was the aftereffects of my near death experience. Most near death experiencers become less materialistic and less worried about status and ambition. It also made it hard to relate to people who mostly talk about their purchases or were planning to buy. Or drama as they engaged in power struggles.

Ninth House: Spirituality: Addict. This is kind of a tough combination to understand. Yet, in another way it makes sense. Although I have some characteristics of the traditional addict personality such as having been a workaholic, I was more of an addict with my spiritual practices after my near death experience. The near death experience started me on a quest for finding how to get back to that incredible peaceful feeling I had on the other side, and for my purpose in life. Perhaps being a spiritual addict is how I survived childhood. Of course, as a child I had not learned about spirituality, I just knew how to accept comfort from the Other Side. Also my mother gave me individual attention, that I cherished, as she supported and believed in the psychic messages that I relayed to her.

I've had both clinical depression and spiritual depression, since I had many losses in my life. It's difficult to say which type triggered which depression. Clinical depression probably came first in my adolescence. Then the near death experience gave me hope and a purpose for living. The book, <u>Heading Towards Omega</u> states near-death experiencers come back to life with an urgency to heal childhood. My second marriage forced me to relive the instant replay of trauma memories from childhood. Angry at God, I temporarily lost my faith. However, when I regained my faith, I got caught up in making emotional and spiritual healing a priority. This priority led to overzealous spiritual practices which made me neglect the rest of life, which then caused poverty and poor health.

The resultant material losses led to clinical depression. I used to meditate, fast, and eat too healthy with observing Ausar Auset Society Church spiritual group practices. Without spiritual guidance from a guru or mentor, I don't know whether my physical disabilities came from poor self-care or were a result of the years I did metaphysical practices. Now I am more balanced and peaceful, determined not to go to any extremes with anything.

Tenth House: Highest Potential: Victim. Whoa! How did the Victim end up in my Tenth House: Highest Potential? I suppose it fits. It could even be comforting to know that there is some explanation for the victim role being so strong in this lifetime and several other past lives. In this lifetime it started with being a Wounded Child and taken on a passive role from there. Initially I did not know any other way to be. Gradually survival instincts taught me. And sometimes other people role-modeled how not to be a Victim for me. Except that, I couldn't understand why other people, especially other women criticized me for not staying in bad situations. Whether on jobs or at places of worship or in relationships I don't know why we try to hold each other down. After my second husband and going to therapy, I refused to go backwards to how I was before for anybody! This recovery started in 1988 and I've been making major changes ever since. Change is not easy, especially with fear of the unknown and possible loss of people and belongings. But going backwards, giving up who I am for other people, is even more frightening. It is a constant struggle, however, it got easier with time.

Coming back from Zimbabwe was when the major tests started. In Zimbabwe, I felt free and whole with amazing unconditional love for the first time in my adult life. I vowed I would bring this love back with me.

Instead, I lost my health and status in the community. My friends at the Ausar Auset Society Church were expecting me to be the same as I was two years prior being able to provide physical labor. They couldn't see or understand my pain and fatigue both physically and emotionally. They were confused, and so was I, about how much I changed.

Unable to obtain employment I became homeless.

I sought help from doctors, but after a while I refused to be in the Victim role, to not continue to spend my precious time waiting long hours for transportation, worried and angry because of what doctors have or haven't done. Humiliated frequently because of the lack of care that uninsured and Medicaid and Medicare patients receive. I had a doctor fuss at me in 1999, when I complained of painful swollen knees and cramps in my left lower back. She said, I've seen knees more swollen than yours. You're one of those women who doctor shop."

A couple of months later I was in the hospital for 10 days, on intravenous antibiotics, unable to keep food down, a fever with a urinary tract infection and brown colored urine. On the day that they discharged me from the hospital, one of the doctors told me that if the other doctors had done the surgery that they were considering then, I probably wouldn't have made it off the operating table!

Several more years of doctors ignoring me, not knowing what to do with me, eventually taught me that I better to be my own healer.

It was only years later, that I was able to become aware of the many ways in all areas of my life where I could be sucked into complaining as a victim. A therapist asked me, "Why did you stay waiting for your friend to come? You could have left at any time. There is no sense in waiting for anyone any longer than 15 minutes."

Unfortunately, we are in the habit of waiting and waiting for others to do something or another, often knowing full well it's probably not ever going to happen. Therefore waiting becomes a convenient excuse. With time and experience, I learned I could refuse to be the victim, and instead reach out towards recognizing my own potential.

Eleventh House: Relationship to The World: Rescuer. I originally chose the Rescuer as one of my shadow archetypes. I was the rescuer with my husbands. They were not the knight in shiny armor that came to whisk me away to be married happily after. However, when I read the meaning of the Eleventh house I felt better identifying with the positive aspects of the rescuer. The Rescuer is able to assist when needed in a crisis or a difficult situation but when the crisis is over is able to withdrawal further help. Initially provide the support, strength and wisdom to help the person gain their own inner strength to carry-on. For years, I definitely have been giving people the tools, and teaching them to fish or provide or solve problems for themselves, and hopefully they will reach out and do the same for someone else. This way the world becomes a better place as everyone cares and shares what they have and know. Some people even have gotten upset because I won't do what they can do themselves, for them. I encourage them do it so that they experience letting go of their fears and gaining self-confidence. Later they thank me. Rescuers are often women. Knights of course are men. Either way, have to be careful to not keep a person dependent on you, especially with an underlying motive of fulfilling your own needs, or for pursuing a romantic relationship. I do tend to want to establish ongoing friendships and can be sad when it's over.

Twelfth House: The Unconscious: Artist. My mother introduced me to all different kinds of arts and crafts when I was a young child. So I've always been an artist. Drawing, crafts, needlework, knitting, crocheting, embroidery, sewing, designing clothes and furnishings, creative writing and watercolor painting. I'm also a cook and a baker. My overall well-being is very much improved when I am being creative.

Creativity and artwork are a form of meditation for me. I enjoyed the inspiration for projects that used to wake me up at 3 o'clock in the morning. I would return to sleep, waking up later at 5 o'clock to go into my sewing room and work until what I dreamed manifested in my hands. Artwork was also a way to find meaning and sanity during the stress of life traumas. I rarely get artistic ideas in the middle of the night these days.

My artistic abilities were still there, but I think intellectual and societal pressure "to get it right" in order to make it "marketable" blocked my creative flow. While living at my aunt's house, I bought books and followed the instructions for entering contests and submitting my watercolor paintings to art galleries, paying entry and shipping fees to unknown places across the country to the West Coast and even up to Canada. When my paintings didn't sell, I had to pay the shipping them back to me.

The best paintings I've done were those that were divinely guided. As if an unseen presence was moving my paint brush across the watercolor paper. The same happened in the past when writing letters to friends and family. It was as if my pen was moving by itself. I've longed for the flow to return. Part of the problem is I think I have become more grounded in this Earth plane than I used to be. Most of my inspiration now comes from images in my meditations more often than nighttime dreams. One of my goals was to paint the endless fields of brilliant red flowers, that I see whenever I close my eyes giving me so much comfort, peace, and joy. These flower images are a reminder of what I saw during my near death experience. I especially see and feel this peace and love as I drift off to sleep after praying for guidance. I wanted to share this comfort, peace and joy with others when they look at my paintings.

However, learning how to paint the illusion of distance and the landscape was very challenging. I bought and read books to aid my learning how to do this faster. Perhaps relying on instructions from books also contributes to artist block. Previously, I did paint a picture of the Inspiration Café, where somehow the geometric perspective of the large dining room was just right.

On a positive note, books now help me work in quicker, more efficient ways for example using various large paintbrushes for special effects, that were less painful for my hands and my back and therefore allowed me to continue to paint. I taught myself how to sketch and paint reclined in my bed or in my wheelchair, similar to how I was to later learn the famous painter Frida Kahlo did.

It occurred to me, while reading the meaning of the Twelfth House, that some of my occasional artist blocks might also be due to fear of what doors may open as my artwork begins to flow.

Could I feel safe enough to surrender? And be free for the rest of my life?

I did continue to paint and gained confidence. People who view my watercolor paintings say they can "feel them, can feel the spiritual energy."

Chapter 14: More Guidance with Sacred Contracts Cards

You can use your personal Sacred Contract archetypal wheel and cards to seek guidance and insight into your thinking and behavior in a situation that you are concerned about.

Working Chart: Moving On

Open to guidance on moving forward with my life, I inquired about moving from Aunt Gussie's home after she died, to an assisted living group home in another suburb. The twelve archetype cards were shuffled and randomly matched to the following houses.

My personal reflections on my thoughts and life are based on both the descriptions and purpose of each House as well as the Archetype in that House. When I journal my spiritual guidance readings, I write or type the meaning of each House and Archetype nearly word-by-word so that it is accessible to me all in one place, when I review it later. I, of course, can't do that here in my published book due to limited space and copyrights. Therefore, please refer to the book, <u>Sacred Contracts,</u> for a fuller understanding and to make your own Archetype Wheel Chart of Origin, and later Working Charts, if you are interested.

First House: Ego Personality: Saboteur. The Saboteur has presented disruptions recently, definitely shaking up my life like an earthquake!

Inside me, I've probably wanted these situations to be disrupted due to uncertainty, boredom, and restlessness, while knowing intuitively that it is time for me to move on. For sure, I have anxieties about the First House representation of all the basic survival needs in life — food, a home, and belonging to a community. Haven't been able to find a local affordable apartment in a reasonable amount of time, which means settling for an assisted living residence back in the city away from family and friends. I worry about having enough money and food to eat. This high anxiety tempts me to take the easy way out and accept my cousin's offer to continue living alone in my aunt's home. Reading about the Saboteur as an ally to warn us to save us from making the same mistakes over and over again, helped me to reconsider. I think if I stayed here, I may be making the mistake of putting myself in the position of hexagram 56: The Wanderer, if told I have to leave at a short notice again. And I would probably honestly hate being in another roommate situation. Would I be sabotaging my own spiritual growth being a Hermit who prefers having my own apartment? People are concerned about me not getting out and doing things, yet they are worried about my safety when I do venture out on my own. Or fuss at me for asking them to do tasks "my way." Yes, I've been afraid of more drastic changes, but I have to be about to dream of better.

Second House: Life Values: Artist. I definitely struggle with the questions, "Now that I'm here, what's mine? And what do I want out of life?" I'm currently challenged with where does my power lie, when I have to rely on others for my physical care. With my own home I would have more say. Being unemployed, using a wheelchair has really decreased my status in society. Overtime, I put aside my previous personal values, rather than be disappointed and argue with people, and I lost my desire to creatively problem solve due to feeling that this is not really my home or my life.

Art is what I usually do in one form or another. When not doing art, I feel empty, somewhat worthless, without an identity. Art is tangible and people challenge me to do more of the Second House external values of money, status, and power in society. Last year, I struggled with my self-worth while facing obstacles trying to promote my watercolor paintings as family pressured me to make use of my college degrees and creativity. I did my best as I invested in computer, printer, scanner, software, books to be able to work from home from my bed even as I taught myself how to use a voice recognition program that typed as I talked. Never lazy, I kept busy.

I've been visualizing and hoping the assisted living residences will allow me to continue to be as independent as possible, help provide for my basic needs, yet give me the freedom to do art. The brochure states the assisted living residence has shelves and cabinets that lower to wheelchair height with the touch of a button, and roll in shower, writing classes, workshops on starting own business, or outside employment, access to parks and transportation.

Third House: Self-Expression Siblings: Hermit. My having gotten used to being immersed in solitary activities and time alone like a Hermit has kept me away from my siblings. However, I do blossomed in community living situations, enjoying the teamwork, as well as when I've ventured away from home and people close to me. Except for living here with Aunt Gussie, I didn't like having roommates because I need my own space to retreat, reflect and recharge. This frees me up to really be myself, enough to give of my talents to the community. It is important to me to maintain contact and closeness with my siblings and friends. My three helpers, who were Aunt Gussie's friends for years have become my friends and I don't know how I would have coped emotionally without their support and guidance. The challenge will be to keep a balance between my need to express myself as an individual, with some controls over my environment, yet not feel that I have to control others in order to have this, or to allow others to control me.

Fourth House: Home: Judge. Well, since my concern is about wanting to have a home, but will likely have to decide on living in an assisted living residence with others, I'm curious what role my Judge archetype has to do with Home. It's true many of my memories and emotions from my past experiences with home environments are a mixture of some joys and sadness. Childhood homes went from fun to frequent relocating, to chaos and abuse. Happily living in Zimbabwe followed by years of moving from place to place, I am now forced to leave yet another happy living situation with my family. Of course, I am afraid of more losses and instability. Writing in my journal, answering the questions of this working chart helps to relieve some of my depression and gives me more energy and optimism.

With the Judge archetype I am more critical and judgmental of myself than others. This probably came from the harsh criticism I received as a child. I've gotten better over the past few months, too exhausted and frustrated to be too hard on myself or others. Although this is some relief from this realization, there is some lingering guilt and sense of failure. In a sense, this could be a form of surrender in a positive way, as I let go of old habits.

Fifth House: Creativity Good Fortune: Addict. I look forward to moving out on my own, and hopefully at the assisted living place as an opportunity to return to spontaneity and abundance. A place to use my creativity, intelligence and imagination. The challenge would be to not base my self-worth on having or not having a professional career. Sometimes I lean towards acceptance that the accomplishments I've done so far in my life are enough, I've worked very hard. However, I honestly yearn to be able to do some of the things I used to do for satisfaction, self-esteem and validation.

I guess where the Addict fits in my personality, is that my creativity was done to excess in the past. One spiritual advisor told me that my overproduction of knitted and sewing items was like my father's excessive procreation. I didn't understand what she meant at the time. It's true that artwork was my escape and release to forget about my problems I had with my marriage, exploitive jobs, and inability to have children. I could ignore these situations and continue to put up with situations, that I should have left or confronted.

Sixth House: Occupation Health: Slave. Past employment contributed immensely to my current health problems because I did not know how to balance work and health. The Slave archetype, which I explained in greater detail in my Chart of Origin has a strong influence on my attitude towards employment as an occupation. As an African American Black women, I've been treated as "a slave" on the job, as well as at home and in the church. The American worker is expected to, more than ever, to do the job of several people, by working long hours plus take work home with them for less pay and benefits. In addition to sacrificing time away from family and friends and community, this makes me a Hermit when I'm at home. A part of me dreads the idea of having to constantly push my body, mind, and spirit over the edge, ever again. Actually, it's a terrifying thought! Yet I miss the income, status, and possibilities of more choices. Hopefully, the assisted living residence fulfills its promises of helping us to obtain gainful employment.

Seventh House: Marriage Relationship: Prostitute. My biggest challenge to moving on is the fear of the loss of close friends, family and partnerships with doctors. Not since I left Philadelphia as a child, and much later while in Zimbabwe, have I had such close friends and contact with family. So precious to me that this fear is enough to paralyze me. The lesson of the Prostitute archetype is to ask ourselves, "How much are we willing to sell, of our core being, to have financial security or to survive?"

Tearful as I write this, because when Aunt Gussie's health started declining, she didn't tell us she was suffering. This put pressure on me as I observed her, to be strong and not give in. I knew from my own experiences and inner truth, that I could no longer live the life of the superwoman trying to please everyone, bearing the blame for everything. I had to do my own soul searching and along the way be myself, to allow Aunt Gussie to have the courage to be herself. We learned a lot from each other that way — in a very short amount of time.

After Aunt Gussie's death, there was a lot of confusion and conflicts among family members. This is usual behavior as people process their grief differently. It was hard to think straight, to do what was right. For a couple of days, I was paralyzed by the shock of the chaos, causing me to have flashbacks to the chaos and abuse I experienced in childhood. When I realized this was happening to me, I was able to rally with others, putting our fears and personal interests aside for the good of the whole, then came peace and better solutions.

Otherwise, my survival was threatened by a desperate need for a place to live. Initially, I had to decide what I was willing to sacrifice of my belongings and finances. Later, my personal integrity was at risk. Tired from all the trauma, I wanted to do what seemed the easy way out. But it was time to "take up my bed and walk" away. Sometimes, I imaged literally having to walk — giving up my wheelchair to have my freedom.

Earlier when I saw that the Prostitute in the seventh house of my Working chart, I procrastinated reflecting and journaling because I thought the Prostitute meant bad news. However, now I'm encouraged because it all makes better sense to me now.

Eighth House: Other Peoples Resources: Amateur. One of the reasons I was almost forced to move suddenly, was some of my cousins arguing over Aunt Gussie's belongings and inheriting the proceeds from selling the house. I wasn't interested in other people's possessions or inheritance even when my father died a decade earlier. Instead, before living in Chicago, I was used to having my own money and control over my finances. However, I am an amateur when it comes to legal and business affairs, and will have to ask questions and do research especially before signing a contract with the assisted living residence. It boasts about having a business center that will train and employ people with disabilities to do medical billing. Since I'm a registered nurse, this would be easier for me.

Ninth House: Spirituality: Wounded Healer. Over this past year, I've done better with integrating spirituality with material interests. Having suffered with several recent losses, I have reasons to be clinically depressed. It could also be more of a spiritual crises, as I hunger to know what to do with my life now, and to connect to my purpose and intuition again. Rereading about the Wounded Healer reminds me that the neurologist diagnosed me with a rare neuromuscular disease for which there is no conventional cure. Frustrating, as I spent years seeking help from doctors, attempting to to have some minimum illusion of control. Symbolic of the frightening realization that I don't have control over my life now either.

As a wounded healer, I've been steadily working on healing emotionally too with a psychotherapist, and making the life changes accordantly by following the spiritual guidance interpretations from the I Ching and other oracles to the best of my understanding. Hopefully, I am coming to the end of the initiation and dark night of the soul required to become a less wounded healer.

Tenth House: Highest Potential: Rescuer. Would I be willing to make the necessary sacrifice, to leave a large part of my life behind to take the opportunity to pursue inner transformation? Yes, I could share my belongings with someone less fortunate than I, who may be coming out of a nursing home, or who I could assist with caregiving. Caretaking is what I've done most of my adult life. Some people took advantage of my kindness.

This is because I did not know at that time that I was a shadow Rescuer (commonly known as codependent). I gave to receive recognition and "love" that was rarely reciprocated. I felt resentful and hurt after awhile. Later, I realized after the divorce, that during the marriage I wasn't allowing my husband to do much giving. I often didn't ask for help, preferring to do without if I couldn't do it myself. Therefore, I couldn't put all the blame on him or anyone else. With time, I started to obtain a balance between being a shadow Rescuer and healthy Rescuer who is able to help individuals to survive through a crisis, then gradually withdraw to allow them to stand on their own feet. As also a Wounded Healer, I need to follow the advice of waiting to be asked to help. Conversely, I have been in the position of being "rescued." After a while my roommate resented me being there because I overstayed my welcome, and in my depression didn't know what to do to help myself because I'd previously always been employed. Moving to an assisted living residence will certainly test my faith.

Eleventh House: Relationship to The World: Victim. I have mixed feelings about my sense of power and the future of humanity. I used to be pretty optimistic in spite of challenges, only allowing myself to cry or feel down for a day or two. However, with recent losses and uncertainty it is difficult to be patient and enthusiastic. Instead, I fear the assisted living situation could put me in the position of the Victim. If I were my usual optimistic self, I would remember and know that I've been blessed in previous, tougher situations that most other people would say wouldn't be possible. When man says, "No." God provides. Being at the assisted living residence could give me a new start. I can learn to set better boundaries with people.

Twelfth House: The Unconscious: Wounded Nature Child. Over the years, I'm gradually learning to be aware of and to trust my intuition. At the age of seven, I began turning off my natural intuition due to abuse. There after followed an abusive marriage as I didn't know how to use my intuition to protect me. I did get away eventually, but it took me awhile, however not as long to get away as other women I knew. This history of childhood abuse and losses gave me a fear of abandonment yet again. Although family members have been supportive and tried to right the situation, it has felt like a dark night of my soul, as I'm exhausted by now. Sometimes, I feel that others who have not gone through what I've gone through, would not understand. I wondered if I was putting on unconscious blinders that may have me ignoring warnings from my intuition, in regards to the reality of living here at my aunt's house or moving to the assisted living residence. Too exhausted to think clearly, no much else to do but surrender spiritually my fears from my childhood, and trust that all will be well, the ultimate task of the twelfth house.

The beautiful colorful birds like the cardinals, along with squirrels, and I will miss Aunt Gussie putting leftover food outside on the air conditioner by the kitchen window, for them and other little creatures who amazing ate together in peace. The squirrels got so used to her routine that they would come one by one and tap on the backdoor if she was late. I used to tease her, that she was turning the squirrels into junk food junkies because they loved french fries. Sometimes, I bought bird seeds and peanuts in the shell for them. The assisted living group home is located near an arboretum. An arboretum is a large garden devoted to growing and studying varieties of trees and shrubs. And of course, birds, squirrels and other creatures would thrive there too, satisfying my need and love of nature.

Change already rearranged my familiar world, as a result of the choices I made at the crossroads over the past year, or more, to pursue my life. I do look to the future as I desperately want my own place so that I can use my talents, such as leaving a legacy of inspirational autobiographies and artwork, heal and be of service to others.

The Sacred Contract cards were new to me during this time. In later years, I could simply look at the archetypes' placement on the wheel chart and immediately understand the meaning as applied to a specific situation seeing myself and my behavior. So obvious, I'd chuckle. Otherwise, the Sacred Contract cards are not as useful for making decisions, as much as helping me examine my thinking, opening me to better clarity and hope.

Her son did eventually allow me to stay at Aunt Gussie's house after she passed on, until I found another place to stay.

Chapter 15: Where Else to Go?

A new Supportive Living apartment building was under construction and available sooner than the other assisted living residence that had a long waiting list. I sought guidance insight into situation of moving to Supportive Living apartments: I Ching hexagram 20 Contemplation (lines 1, 4, and 6) into hexagram 17 Following. Metu Neter cards: Maat tem tchaas/ Amen hetep.

I Ching hexagram 20 Contemplation is, of course, about contemplating a situation before taking action, going beyond a narrow perspective similar to "looking through a keyhole." Doing deep meditation for better insights. Also warns that when observing others know that they are also observing you. Line 1: Go ahead and do it although you may not understand the whole situation, you will benefit. Line 4: treat others with respect. Remember to consult the oracles regularly and follow this guidance with respect. Line 6: Have to view this situation from a much higher spiritual perspective of seeing the interconnected whole of society and the universe. Beyond blame and hurt. Have to consider the effects we each have on each other. Hexagram 17 Following: is when someone more experienced helps someone less experienced. Usually this is an elder. Learning to share and serve others. It also means following the natural cycles and laws of the universe. Understand and follow your destiny reading incarnation objective. Surround oneself with good people and stay away from bad influences.

Metu Neter cards: Maat tem tchaas/ Amen hetep. Remember that abundance comes from heaven. By establishing inner peace in the situation, it will change for the better.

There were many challenges, even before I moved into Supportive Living apartments. I will briefly summarize it here, because as I was reviewing my daily journals from 2004-2005, I realized that even one month of the unbelievable events that happened there will not fit in this book. When I applied in November

2004, it was under construction. Their representatives explained that supportive living facilities are similar to assisted living places for seniors, except it was for younger people ages 22 to 64 years-old. They got me excited by telling me about having my own one-bedroom apartment along with amenities of a movie theater, computer and fitness rooms. I was to choose my apartment from three different floor plans.

In February, they called to tell that me I had to share it with a roommate. March brought more disappointment as they told me the building wouldn't be ready for another three weeks. April rolled on by too. Finally, I moved in May to a tiny two-bedroom apartment. To discover that my bedroom, as another resident described it, was the "size of a 7'x 11' jail cell." Mind you, this is supposed to be a place for young adults with physical disabilities. My hospital bed barely fit. Transferring from my wheelchair to the bed and out was a struggle. I had to give away a lot of my belongings and put the rest in storage downstairs. What were they thinking when they chose and designed this place? There were pillars inside the apartments that further chopped the living space even smaller!

Food was served restaurant style initially when we first arrived. Fabulous menu with at least three entree selections at each meal. By June, they were serving us mostly pastas where you had to search for the sauce and the meat. As you can imagine, this did not work for me because I couldn't eat gluten foods. I ate the salads and fruit plates when available. Many days, I went hungry.

Although a nurse came out to our homes prior to us moving to Supportive Living and assessed our individual needs, making sure that our total score did not add up to requiring too much care or too little care, soon after we got there, their nurse told us that we had to be independent, to able to take care of ourselves. I was already taking care of myself, living alone but my doctor wanted me to get some rest and not have to worry about unreliable home care aides. Ha, ha, ha. I guess we both were dreaming.

Money equals independence. With Supportive Living taking our whole

Social Security checks, even if some resident's checks were over $1400 a month, and then only giving us $90 to live off of, we were supposed to be excited because if we were in a nursing home, we would only get $35! Maybe glad, except soon after we saw Supportive Living was not providing services — resentment and panic set in. Paying for telephone service and a shared cable bill for internet and television took up most of the $90. Couldn't go anywhere without bus fare, and they had minimal activities and outings for us. Although we had a little "kitchen" in each apartment, basically a one burner cooktop and a small refrigerator, management later asked us to give Supportive Living our food stamps! We couldn't even buy snacks?

It was difficult not to complain, blame and not feel hurt, especially since living there was better than being homeless. I tried to make the best of the situation. There were of course some good benefits to living there. Instead of living alone and feeling lonely, we make friends and visited each other in the dining room or in each other's rooms. I put together an art group for other residents and taught them art techniques adapted to each person's disability. For example, there were a couple of people who were blind, that I helped to do watercolor paintings.

James found me at the Supportive Living apartments. I was surprised to see him. He gave me more of his large beautiful paintings, that I had encouraged him to do back when we were both living in homeless transitional housing. James had moved further north to his own apartment. The reason why my family hadn't seen him for a while, is because he was having health problems.

When I couldn't bare the conditions at Supportive Living anymore, is after a night in July, when I had trouble breathing. In the morning I went in my wheelchair to the emergency room several blocks away. I prayed all the way there. We were all afraid to go to the hospital because a lot of our apartment mates did not come back. They were transferred to nursing homes instead.

Sitting up, my breathing was easier, therefore the ER doctors didn't believe my distress during the night.

Subsequently they did not admit me or even keep me long enough for observation. They didn't know what to do with me. Previously when I lived with my aunt, I had good doctors out in the suburbs who knew me. Prayed all the way back to Supportive Living. The nearer I wheeled down the sidewalks to the Supportive Living place, the harder I prayed to have my own apartment since I had to take care of myself anyway. No nurses checked on me. Being at Supportive Living had me sicker because I couldn't take care of myself, the way I knew was best for my health.

My prayers were answered the very next day! One and a half years prior, I applied for senior housing. The manager had called a month ago and told me that I was number eleven on the list, and asked was I still interested? I wasn't enthusiastic as I said, "Yes" because I had applied for other housing too, five years earlier and I hadn't heard from any of them.

Now, when this manager asked, "There is an apartment available. Do you want it?

Of course, I said, "Yes!"

A bit fearful though, because again I was saying "Yes" to an apartment that I hadn't seen.

Chapter 16: Home?

Oracle readings for moving to the senior apartment building:

Hexagram 7 The Army (lines 1 and 5) into hexagram 60 Limitations.

Hexagram 7 The Army: Line 1: Must begin with everything in proper order. If not organized, then failure. Line 5: Must have an experienced leader. Punishment is justified but not excessively.

Hexagram 60 Limitations. Usually means the need for self-limitations and self-discipline.

Metu Neter cards: Ausar tem Maat/ Auset tu maat

After another night of being awake, my alarm clock rang at 5:50 AM, because if we did not call the paratransit companies close to 6:00 A.M then all the rides would already be taken. I was grateful and amazed that the paratransit ride reservationist answered the phone on my third attempt, so I could make arrangements for my ride to the apartment interview. After I hung up the phone and made myself comfortable in my bed, I realized I've been saying, "If I were at home, I would make pizza with rice crust and mozzarella soy cheese. If I were at home, I would eat what I wanted to eat, whenever I wanted to eat If I were at home, I would have items I need within easy reach. If I were at home, I would rest when I need to rest, without having to try to explain to the staff why in order to get my needs met."

If I am saying, "If I were at home. If I were at home, if I were at home, then that means I'm not at home. So where is home? Is there a home for me?"

Some of the anxiety and panic I felt is fear that when I move out, that it won't be home, same as being here in Supportive Living is not home for me. There's so much wrong here, that it is difficult to imagine anywhere else being better. Who will help me unpack? If I don't get unpacked immediately, how long before the real apartment feels like home? Will I have a responsible, compassionate, intuitive helper? Will she understand and help me even when I look "well?"

A Jehovah's Witness friend of my grandmother called me. She gave me inspiration by telling me, "When you pray, you need to be specific. What did you pray for before you moved to assisted-living?

"Well, I did ask for plenty of sunshine coming through the windows. That I got. The people are good here except for the management."

"I'll pray for you too, that you have a peaceful home and peace in your heart, in the meantime. You shouldn't have to live in a place that you hate. Home should be where you can close the door and be safe and peaceful. I'm shocked that you have a roommate, and she's a stranger to you. It will be good that you have someplace to look forward to moving to."

She had called to ask me for my grandmother's phone number, but I'm glad she talked to me and was very understanding of my situation. She recently moved to a lovely senior citizen apartment in a far southwest suburb to be near her children.

But what are the specifics to ask Great Mama for my new apartment? Confused now because Supportive Living "promised" many other things I asked for prior to moving there. So now I decided to pray for: a wheelchair accessible apartment with large enough doorways, bathroom, toilet and shower. Plenty of closets and storage space with a linen closet, bedroom closets, storage closet, and foyer closet. Space for bookshelves, cabinets, file cabinet and that the kitchen cabinets are large enough. Space for medical equipment and medicine. That there is proper space around my BiPAP machine for airflow, distilled water with medications close by. A real kitchen with a large refrigerator and freezer, double sink, and plenty of counter space. An art room with plenty of space for creativity, to set up my watercolor painting easel and sewing machine. Plenty of insulated large breathable windows that let in sunshine and gives me a view of green trees and gardens.

Tomorrow arrived. The apartment manager opened the main door for me and told me to wait in the TV room, while the assistant manager finished her lunch. There was an older woman, seventy-eight years old which she proudly told me, in the TV room. She quizzed me with many personal questions. Usually I'm offended by people asking me personal questions, but I curiously answered her.

"Are you married?"

"No. I was."

"Why didn't you stay married? He could've taken care of you. Do you have anyone to come in and clean for you? How old are you? You don't look any older than twenty-seven. Why don't you dye your hair black? Your hair is more salt than pepper on the top."

The benefits of tolerating her questioning is that she told me some things about the apartment building.

"I live on 11th floor. I have a beautiful apartment. But it is cold in the winter with snow on the roof, and hot in the summer with the sun beaming on the roof. There's an area out in the back with benches. There are a lot of Russians here. They don't speak English and they stay to themselves. Who told you about here?"

"A young woman told me. Actually she begged me to put in an application, although they use a lottery system meaning they may or may not pull my number.

"Is she Black?"

"No, I met her in a group we belong to."

I was glad when the assistant apartment manager called me into the manager's office. She and the manager also thought I was too young, in my twenties.

"No, I'm closer to fifty years old."

"We wondered since this is a senior building, although we do accept some mature adults with disabilities."

The interview mostly consisted of signing a lot of papers.

"HUD will let us know in two to three weeks. So since you have to give the Supportive Living place thirty days' notice, September 1st would probably be your move-in date."

I told myself, 'all is as it should be', even though I am a little impatient that it took two weeks already for me to receive the certified letter, then another week because the assistant manager was on vacation. It could've been that, in that amount of time I would have had approval, and had given my 30 day notice by now. But heaven knows best; like why did I have to detour to the assisted living place first, and what was my purpose there?

She took me up on the elevator to the third floor to see a vacant apartment, which she explained would not be my apartment because mine would be a wheelchair accessible apartment. Basically all of the apartments there were the same size and layout. She opened the white folding closet door on the left. I was pleased at the length and tall height of the closet. Behind me, she showed me another closet that was for hanging coats. There was another door next to it and I was amazed that it was a continuation of the same long closet! The kitchen is a real kitchen! There are cabinets on two walls with upper and lower cabinets plus more on the breakfast island. Plenty countertops. A real refrigerator with a large freezer and large electric stove! The sink is not double, but it is large enough for a dishpan with space on the side to rinse dishes. In the large bedroom there is also a large long closet. I moved into the senior apartment building on August 31, 2005 and have been living here ever since.

My understanding of the reading was that the senior apartment building would provide my own independent space to heal (Auset). My health initially imposed the hexagram 60 self-limitations. Hexagram 7 (line 1) is similar to a disciplined army structure where everything needs to be in proper order.

Line 5 means punishment needs to be given out to someone who has transgressed against you. The Supportive Living director was inexperienced, as it was the first assisted living apartments designed for young adults with disabilities. His heart was right, but he used deception with us. Therefore he needed to be punished for his transgressions. I didn't do any punishing though.

I moved into the senior apartment building on August 31, 2005.

Books and Articles Mentioned in This Book

I purposely did not write this book in a scholarly way, with huge academic words, book quotes and citations. This is because we all have this knowledge and information within us. Books are just one way to share and communicate with each other. I believe there really is no such thing as an expert, it is simply one person sharing their opinion and experiences. The so-called expert may have done the research and statistics to find how many other people might agree. And they had the money and the time to get published. But life is always changing. Meaning what was true two weeks ago, may not be true today. And the authors may live in a completely different situation than yours, and therefore the advice may make no sense for your current life situation. Books are a way to have a long-distance conversation, often with a stranger. But there is enough commonalities so that we don't feel alone.

Decisions Decisions: Getting Answers to Life's Challenges: Volume 1 Getting Started. By Haneefa Mateen (2023).

I Ching: A New Interpretation for Modern Times. By Sam Reifler (1974).

I Ching: The Tao of Drumming. By Michael Drake. (1991). Talking Drum Publications. (paperback). Random House Publishing Group. (e-book).

I Ching Praxis: Forty Years of Practical Insights into the I Ching. By Ra Un Nefer Amen (2014). Khamit Media Trans Visions, Inc.

Light Emerging: The Journey of Personal Healing. By Barbara Ann Brennan. (1993). Bantam Books.

Metu Neter Cards. By Ra Un Nefer Amen (1990). New York, Khamit Corporation.

Metu Neter Vol. 1: The Great Oracle of Tehuti and the Egyptian System of Spiritual Cultivation. By Ra Un Nefer Amen (1990). New York, Khamit Corporation.

Mother's Love from Beyond: A Healing Journey of Grief and Loss: A Memoir. By Haneefa Mateen. (2021).

Sacred Path Cards: The Discovery of Self through Native Teachings. By Jamie Sams (1990). New York: HarperCollins Publishers.

Sacred Path Workbook: New Teachings and Tools to Illuminate Your Personal Journey. By Jamie Sams (1991). New York: HarperCollins Publishers.

The Astrology of I Ching. (1976, 1993). By W. K. Chu and W. A. Sherrill. Penguin Books.

The I Ching or Book of Changes. By Richard Wilhelm and Cary Baynes. (1950). Princeton University Press.

The Illustrated I Ching Workbook. R. L. Wing. (1987). Aquarian Press.

Author's Bio

Haneefa Mateen has a wealth of life experiences and knowledge from exploring healing methods for mind, body and soul. A natural teacher, healer, and artist she shares more of her wisdom. Her books are accessible, easy on the eyes, available in large print format.

She has an associate's degree in registered nursing, bachelor's in International Studies, master's in Rehabilitation Counseling, and a doctorate in Clinical Psychology. She currently does spiritually integrated therapy and healing, and is active in

African American community cultural events.

www.ingramcontent.com/pod-product-compliance
Lightning Source LLC
Chambersburg PA
CBHW020525080526
44583CB00013B/741